AN INTRODUCTION TO COMMUNITY WORK

Fred Milson

Head of Community and Youth Service Section
Westhill College of Education, Birmingham

Routledge & Kegan Paul
London and Boston

First published in 1974
by Routledge & Kegan Paul Ltd
Broadway House, 68-74 Carter Lane,
London EC4V 5EL and
9 Park Street,
Boston, Mass. 02108, USA
Set in Monotype Plantin
and printed in Great Britain by
Clarke, Doble & Brendon Ltd, Plymouth
© Fred Milson 1974

ISBN 0 7100 7840 4 (c)
      0 7100 7841 2 (p)

Library of Congress Catalog Card No. 73–92986

To Tom
Son-in-Law and Friend

Contents

Preface

'Community' is a word in frequent use today. A cynic might suppose that we talk about it so much precisely because we have so little of it, just as reforming movements may reach a stage in their historical development where, having nothing left to say, they concentrate attention on how to say it, on the means and techniques of communication rather than on the content. But the cynic is wrong: at least his view is myopic. For whilst there are depressing signs of a partial decay of 'community feeling' and 'community responsibility' in certain situations, yet this is by no means the whole story. Part of the remainder is a concentration in many quarters on the possibilities and opportunities of 'community work' and the hope that it may offer an improvement in the quality of life for millions of the inhabitants of the earth. Social philosophers ponder its meaning: sociologists seek to relate it to their intellectual discipline: politicians assess its influence with the electorate: committees—like the Gulbenkian—meet for years to consider the best method of training for community-work roles: a government department sponsors local schemes to test the ideas in chosen neighbourhoods: 'grass roots' community workers, in increasing numbers, work with neighbourhood groups: local people wait for none of these and form their own tenants' associations and action groups to gain a pedestrian crossing near the school, an adventure playground on an estate or to stop an airport being built in the area: and, not least significant, men and women of many disparate occupations begin to ask themselves whether 'community work' has a powerful meaning for their work—and the list includes teachers, parsons, social workers, architects, planners of various kinds, policemen, doctors and nurses.

In fact it is tempting to react excessively against the cynic's comment, to find all these developments heady stuff and to feel that the tide of democracy is sweeping us on to an active and participant society:

> Bliss were it then to be alive
> But to be young, were very heaven.

Closer contact with the evidence may modify this rapture. Many local schemes of community work prove deeply disappointing on any objective evaluation: indeed, in some cases, by general agreement, 'the last state of that house is worse than the first'. On further inspection, interest in the professions proves to be the enthusiasm of a vocal minority. And, perhaps even more perplexing, there is little coherence among the advocates and practitioners of community work. Many different people, with contrasting intentions and philosophies, shelter under the broad umbrella marked 'community work'.

No less serious is a defect which is also an intriguing paradox. This movement, which aims to be popular in the best sense, has so far failed on the whole to produce a literature that can be understood by 'non-academics', or to develop any other mode of popular communication. So—to put the matter in an extreme caricature—the 'lie' too frequently at the heart of this movement is that though dedicated to citizen involvement in the running of the country, it often turns out to be an élitist group who are saying to the people 'We are determined that you shall participate'. At least that is the strong impression I have received during long attendances at study-group committees.

And yet I for one cannot leave the matter there, since in my view the basic ideas of community work are generous, compassionate, just, sensible and so far inevitable that it seems the future belongs to them.

It is at this point that the purpose of this book can best be described. The writer seeks to do for the reader what he had first to do for himself. When the constellation of ideas associated with the modern use of the term 'community work' first forced themselves upon my attention I had to spend a lot of time answering the question 'What does it all mean?' Part of the answer is this book which aims to be a primer on community work, starting from square one, taking nothing for granted—which is how I proceeded to answer my own dilemmas.

There is another purpose. Most of the people who think and write about community work agree that the enterprise presupposes a 'value system': in other words, community workers, however non-directive they may be in their methods, are making an assumption that some things are better for people than some other things. Undeniably all forms of social intervention—including the work of school-teachers and probation officers—rest on this base. So far so good. But what one rarely finds in 'community work' circles is a discussion about these values, their sanctions and authority. They are usually taken for granted, and hence they are left unexplored, unexamined and ill-defined. One may go so far as to say that, in the present pluralistic climate, 'community work' philosophers are frequently coy about the values implicit in their endeavours. One commentator has described the tone in which these issues are discussed as 'rather like a maiden aunt who fears her niece may drink too much sherry'.

This book, whilst offering no easy answers, explores the main issues and dilemmas implicit in the value assumptions of community work.

The last chapter may easily be misunderstood. It proffers a Christian framework for the human values which lie behind community work. This of course is only for those who can on other grounds accept the main Christian doctrines. It is not designed to convert anybody to anything, my own hold on the faith being too tenuous to support anything of that sort: though what is written there does happen to represent my personal philosophy. But it is an optional extra for the reader. The rest of the book I trust holds up without it. Those who are irritated today by any presentation of religious truth—including a few of my best friends—would do well to ignore it. I hope not to be so far misunderstood as to be thought guilty of crass stupidity. I do not deny that many good community workers operate without this faith: I am proud to work with them: I am far from claiming that these are the only possible sanctions for community-work values. But all of us in community work are operating on value assumptions and none of us can forever put off the time when we examine the credentials and the authority of those value assumptions.

1   What is a community?

The difficulty of definition

'When I use a word', Humpty Dumpty said in a rather scornful tone, 'it means just what I choose it to mean—nothing more and nothing less.' 'The question is,' said Alice, 'whether you can make things mean so many different things.'

We are all familiar with the difficulty. Serious conversation is hindered when the participants use the same word with different meanings. That is a common problem in communication. It may arise from cultural variations. Thus, I am told, that a public speaker in Canada offends his audience if he describes them as 'homely', though the same adjective would not be unacceptable in Britain. But more commonly the hindrance arises between members of the same country and culture. Many promising discussions end in conflict, impasse, confrontation, anger or misunderstanding simply because we never stop to ask the question, 'Are we using words with the same meaning?' Are we—in a significant phrase in everyday use—'talking the same language'? Occasionally the misunderstanding is part of a deliberate mistake used with a joking intention, as in the case of the local councillor who when asked by the YWCA enthusiast whether he was in favour of clubs for women, replied, 'Only when every other means of persuasion has failed'. Comedians on the stage make an extensive use in their patter of the double meaning of words. But more commonly it is unintentional and unconscious yet a serious barrier to human relationships.

This is why we must begin with definitions: we want to be clear about the meaning we attach to several key words in the present discussion.

In common speech, we use the word 'community' to describe a wide variety of social units. Near my home, there is a long road which has its own boys' football team organized by the fathers. 'It is not surprising', somebody said, 'they are a real community down in Etchells Lane.' The same city houses several thousand members of the Jewish faith. They do not live in the same neighbourhood, though many of them gather once a week on the

1

Sabbath at a central synagogue. A parson, asked how many came to his church services, admitted to no large congregations but said, 'You see, we are a community church. We exist to serve the people in the streets around us.' A headmaster may make a similar claim for his school and I know one managing director of a small factory who said the same about his work force. A man who migrates to the city from a small village reports sadly how he misses the old style of living. 'We are a community there.' On the other hand, a councillor in a large city will sometimes refer to it as a community.

These examples serve to show that in everyday speech 'community' is stretched until it simply means 'a number of people who have something in common'.

The popular use of the term in fact contains many confusions and is an example of our muddled thinking: 'community' is one of those words which we are inclined to use frequently, serene in the confidence that we know what it means until somebody asks us to define it. One stereotype, not unaffected by nostalgia, is evoked by Mitford's description of life in a village in the 1820s— 'a little world of our own where we know everyone and are known to everyone, interested in everyone and authorized to hope that everyone is interested in us'.[1] To make sense in the present discussion we should learn a more precise meaning of the word.

When we turn to the sociologists it is disappointing at first to find that they too are not agreed on a meaning. There is here, in fact, so much ambiguity in their writings that a casual student might be forgiven for supposing that the meaning given to 'community' depends entirely on which book he is reading. One investigator looked at ninety-four existing definitions of the word and his disconcerting conclusion was that 'beyond the recognition that "people are involved in community" there is little agreement of the use of the term'.[2]

There are at least four senses in which 'community' may be used, four social realities it may describe. One, the small community, local and with many areas of common life. Two, an association of people with common life who do not live in the same neighbourhood. Three, localized and large but with little common life throughout. Four, a process. There are reasons and excuses for this lack of clear guidance from the appropriate academic discipline. Sociology as a separate study has grown up at a time of rapid social change and has continually adapted to new realities. The emergence of new sociological perspectives and concepts can be traced partly to this fact and also to the general progress and refinement of the subject.

Students often look to social sciences for exact definitions which they can then take over, and perhaps feel that they are henceforth not required to think about for themselves. This might not always be the right expectation. And on this matter of 'community', sociology may, as in other matters, offer us insight, rather than finality. It can compel us to face the central issues involved in making sense of this part of human experience, and thus help us on the way to our own workable definition. This is our approach in the remainder of the chapter.

In the last resort, if all else fails, we can always remind ourselves that, as life is more than any of its categories, 'community' will still represent a dimension of human experience though all attempts at exact definition should fail. We are aware that we belong to two broad types of human association. The first is primary, face-to-face, personal, small and intimate, like the family. The other is secondary, and often impersonal like our town or our national trade union. To many of the latter type we often give the title 'community'. We know the difference between the two types of 'belongingness'—for example in the expectations and support we encounter—even when we cannot be articulate about them. That would be poor consolation for an academic sociologist who is properly concerned about the accurate use of language: but it is more comforting for us whose focus of attention is on the practical features of the subject. Even so, and despite the blurred edges, there is profit for practitioners in asking what are the main issues with which the social scientists have been concerned.

'Folk' models and 'sociological' models

Public opinion is not invariably right. Careful investigation some-times modifies popular judgments on social issues, though on other occasions it confirms and supports them. One mode of expressing this, common in textbooks, is to compare and contrast what are called the 'folk' models and the 'sociological' models. We believe this approach has value in the present context and we propose to apply it in four relevant areas as we move to our working definition.

First, community is not just, and not always a simple, localized unitary reality   One writer[3] on the subject in describing a 'small community' provided criteria which were in vogue for a long time and accurately reflect a common, stereotyped image. Redfield's characteristics were distinctiveness, small size, self-sufficiency and homogeneity of inhabitants. Now of course there are many societies which fit fairly accurately into this description. One such has been described for us by Ronald Blythe.[4] The village of Akenfield scores highly on three of Redfield's tests. It has a separate identity—it can, for example, be clearly distinguished from neighbouring villages: it is small, only a few people live there: and the inhabitants share many attitudes and values and exhibit a general like-mindedness. It scores less highly on the remaining characteristic—self-sufficiency—which is always the weakest part of this kind of typology. Akenfield needs links with other communities to survive as a cultural, social and political reality. Though Redfield has given a fairly accurate account of certain traditional communities, sociologists would question whether even of that kind his descriptions are wholly accurate: but, going further, they would want to question a popular prejudice to use Redfield's model when we think of community. For both misgivings the following are the main reasons.

a   The 'little community' on investigation is found to be made up of different groups: they may not be in conflict, but they will certainly be disparate. Social class differences exist in villages. Goldman found, for example, that this reality considerably impeded youth club work in a small community.[5] Ethnic groups can be seen both in small-town Alabama and the West Midlands of England and their members belong both to the total community and the community of their own people.

b   Communities are rarely examples of a unitary solidarity for another reason. The members' interests and concerns overlap with other communities and there is a penetration into the whole from other communities. A man may travel miles to work or to play squash or to attend an art class in an evening institute. The Baptists and the radio hams and the members of the Women's Institute, and the chess players—to name but a few—will feel that they belong to communities whose boundaries are wider than the small community: national and, perhaps, international. There may not be enough boys in the village to form a football team and co-operation is sought with a neighbouring village. There is a widespread conviction that the self-sufficiency of small communities has been exaggerated in the popular imagination.

c   How far is the idea of 'locality' essential to the notion of 'community'? Are we always referring to a geographical reality when we use the term? Or is it also permissible to speak of 'communities of interest' where there is a shared concern or belief or pursuit or inheritance but all the members do not necessarily inhabit the same area or neighbourhood?

König roundly asserts 'in the strictly sociological sense the phenomenon of spatial proximity of neighbourhood is inseparable from the idea of community'.[6] He is followed by others. But König is also concerned to persuade us to think not merely in geographical and administrative terms but to turn our attention to the social relationships involved in community life.[7]

Most definitions in fact identify the 'residential community' and 'the community of interest', though these overlap. 'Originally the term *community* denoted a collectivity of people who occupied a geographical area. . . . To-day . . . Community, although less all-inclusive, and slightly more specific in connotation, may be regarded as denoting a community of interests.'[8] This is not merely a recognition that the essence of the reality is not guaranteed by geography alone: all communities are societies but not all societies are communities. But it goes further and suggests that there can be 'community' among social groups who do not inhabit the same area. (Or if the purists are to have their way we must find another word to describe this social reality.)

On Sundays at New Street Station, Birmingham, large numbers of Asian citizens crowd the platforms waiting for trains to take them to a central meeting place. They do not all live in the same district yet they are a community in the sense that they share beliefs, culture, problems and a socio-economic position: they are conscious of a relationship, conscious of its limitations and conscious of its differences from other similar relationships. One recent community study has for its constituency the zones which people use in Paris and not merely the areas in which they live.[9]

B

The world-wide Jewish community—scattered through historical circumstances—is an extreme example of a type that is based on beliefs, aspirations, identity and shared threats and not on common residence. Varied titles are given to this species: 'functional', 'spiritual', 'interest', 'moral', 'psychic'.

It is not that the notion of locality has been entirely abandoned. For many people, the immediate neighbourhood is still a decisive factor in their experience and development, second only to the family. The two central notions in the concept remain territorial definition and social separateness. But what has happened is that partly under pressure from modern developments like increased mobility and improvement in communications, the geographical does not dominate the scene so much, and conversely, the inner relationships of community claim more attention. Paradoxically, in modern times we are moving to an emphasis on an older dictionary definition—a body of men having something in common.

d   The notion of 'locality' is a blunt tool in the understanding of *community* and undue reliance upon it will lead to frustration. For not only, as we have seen, are we confronted with human groups which, lacking a local habitation, yet have the characteristics of a community, but there is a further difficulty. Local communities differ from each other in so many ways that we have to employ adjectives lest we be found lumping together things which are very different. The common examples of course are hamlet, small town, large town, city, metropolis. But size of area and population is not the only distinguishing feature: others include the extent, wealth and populousness of the surrounding neighbourhood: the specialized functions of the community within the whole society: the kind of organizations the community has.[10] To include Glasgow and Stow-in-the-Wold, or Mallaig and Beverley in the same categories is to insist that an elephant is like a mouse because they both have four legs. That is true but it is the differences between the two animals which are significant. In assessing the notion of community we need other and more discriminating tools than those marked 'locality'.

The modifications of the popular image suggested in this section would be generally believed to receive powerful reinforcement from the conditions of modern living. There are simply many more associations to which people can belong today. Life in a small community is likely to be less confined. There is far more

overlapping of communities and a man is less likely to be compelled to restrict his associations to the local neighbourhood.
(Some think this process has gone so far that 'there is no longer
community, but only association', but this is a point to be examined later and in more detail.) A man today may well live in one
neighbourhood, work in another, play golf in a third, worship
God in a fourth and play the violin in an orchestra of a nearby
town. In the small isolated seaside village of Sandsend on the
north-east coast of Yorkshire I was told a curious fact. There were
a few men in Sandsend who had never left the village until they
went to Flanders to fight in the First World War. Ease and speed
of travel, social mobility, the growth of the mass media, the
wider distribution of wealth and educational opportunity: these
are some of the factors which in Sandsend, as elsewhere, have
contributed to the making of a very different human situation.
And they are a few of the reasons compelling us to look again at
our common images of *community*.

*Second, the general feeling that 'modern conditions' affect 'community'
has received confirmation from sociological enquiries* For public
opinion is not always consistent: in this matter, it is in a state of
transition: the persistence of stereotyped images of 'community'
as localized and unitary, exists side by side with a widespread
feeling that there has been a disastrous loss of community feeling.
Greenleigh has replaced Bethnal Green. We hear this conviction
expressed in the nostalgic musings of many elderly people. 'It's
not like it was in the old days. People cared, now nobody seems to
care. The neighbours were always popping in to see how you were,
or just to talk. We hadn't very much but we helped each other.'
From different parts of the country come reports of a decline in
community activities: the local agricultural show or the 'well-
dressing' does not attract the support of former times though
working-men's clubs flourish.

Brief reference is made here to four famous theses which, in
scholarly terms, express the same conviction that the twin modern
developments of urbanization and industrialization affect community feeling and action.

Tönnies, writing in the 1870s,[11] contrasted *Gemeinschaft* and
Gesellschaft. The first form of human grouping is marked by
intimate, rich and deeply satisfying relationships. *Gesellschaft*

describes an alliance that is contractual, calculating, impersonal and partial. Though Tönnies thought that neither were found in their pure forms, yet his conclusion was unequivocal and sad. He saw European countries, under the pressure of industrialization, substituting *Gesellschaft* for *Gemeinschaft*. MacIver[12] gave a twentieth-century interpretation to Tönnies's views. He defined community as being a group of people who shared their lives at many points: and an association as an assemblage simply to pursue one interest in a group of interests. 'The difference is obvious: we contrast the business or the church or the club with the village or city or nation.' Between these two lies the powerful influence of Durkheim[13] who, with his characteristic sensitivity to social pressures, saw the division of labour as a prime cause of the change in the common pattern of social cohesion. In a society where more and more men train for specialized work roles, 'mechanical solidarity' (based on like-mindedness) gives way to 'organic solidarity' (marked by individual diversity). No less influential was the work of an American social psychologist at the beginning of this century. Cooley[14] introduced the phrase 'primary groups' which were small enough to allow for a complete network of face-to-face and intimate relationships, being very powerful in forming the social nature and the ideals of the individual: so much so that in speaking of them he is likely to say 'we'. 'One lives in the feeling of the whole, and finds the chief aims of his will in that feeling.' Predictably, subsequent writers referred to 'secondary groups'. A body of belief grew up that industrialized societies multiplied these with a consequent diminution in the number and the power of 'primary groups'. On this view, the individual's experience of 'mass society' replaces more and more the commitment and support of the personalized band. Man, so to speak, knows 'society' more and more and 'community' less and less.

Third, a widespread misgiving that 'industry and the city' have killed 'community feeling' would be questioned by sociological thinking on the subject   That urbanization, industrialization and bureaucratization have profoundly affected human experience in our era, nobody who ponders the evidence will doubt. But whether the acids of modernity have eaten away the 'body of community' may seriously be doubted. For one thing, a suspicion is abroad that idyllic pictures were painted of the strength of fraternity in English villages in the eighteenth and nineteenth centuries: but longer treatment awaits this topic in the next section. More positively, researches have suggested that it was premature to conclude that primary groups could not flourish, say in the city: nor is a sense of 'neighbourhood' always absent from this setting. Moreover, new patterns of secondary association may form there, valuable because they are relevant, and also an expression of community. A value judgment has occasionally been introduced into the argument at this point. 'Loving your neighbour in a city'—it has been said—may require not rural mateyness but joining large movements to support a struggle to obtain justice for him. On this view, knowing your milkman's name is not as important as, say, refusing to have your daily supplies delivered by a non-union milkman.

Worsley goes so far as to say that the early urban community studies were frustrated because their authors were working with rural models in mind. So long as investigators worked with 'the small community' as a norm they could not see the city shining with its own light. They could not make anything of it whilst they were using the wrong conceptual tools. When this myth was finally abandoned they saw patterns of relationships—even in Vanity Fair—for which at present we have no better word than 'community'.[15]

Fourth, we cannot look to the sociologists as such to be the 'saviours' or even the reformers of mankind   A common expectation is that they will be: we expect them to provide the remedies for our ills, 'to produce the goods': their specialized studies, we feel, should fit them both to describe the contours of Utopia and to land us there. Amongst many people in Britain there is an exaggerated respect for academic achievement and this can still be true of a man who is frequently among his friends a denigrator of the theorists and 'arm-chair critics'. A decade of introducing the subject of sociology to students in a college of education has shown me how prevalent are the moral and messianic expectations of students. An insistence that in the strict discharge of their office sociologists must be 'value-free' is greeted with a mixture of disappointment, unbelief and a suspicion that one is saying that sociologists, as human beings, are immoral. But it has to be said that their function is to say what is and not concern themselves with what ought to be. They can discern patterns in apparently unrelated instances of social behaviour but they have no mandate to pronounce one form of society better than another.

Now, it is quite true that in this respect the cobbler does not always stick to his last. The social thinker dons the mantle of the prophet. Tönnies, for example, was not content to point to the decline of 'community' and the growth of 'association': he became emotional in deploring the trend. A few of the founding fathers of sociology—Weber is a good example—were not willing to sit in their studies or even to be engaged in field research: they were energetic in social action and reforming movements. That is to be expected since sociologists are also human beings involved with their fellows in the struggle for a better life: and a 'value-free' perspective is likely to be an ideal rather than a reality, a self-conscious commitment rather than an unconscious drive. But the fact is that once they move into the practical field they have ceased to act as sociologists: they are now describing what ought to be rather than what is: and as moral and social philosophers they do not have the same authority. A widespread fallacy is that these experts can tell us what we ought to do. This expectation is often unfulfilled. True, they can provide criteria by which we are compelled to re-examine our existing value judgments as when Blythe points out that the village of Akenfield was not simply a 'happy family' but at the 'big house' servants were treated like serfs. But in offering practical programmes the sociologists often display disagreements among themselves and their views on what is right and wrong rarely merits the same attention. Value judgments about what kind of a society we want is a decision for a whole population, ideally based on the advice of moral philosophers and implemented through politicians and community action.

The present use of the word 'community'

Locality

In what follows our attention is almost always on the neighbourhood and the sense of belonging and levels of co-operation which are at least latent and potential in it. Though modern conditions have affected the individual's dependence upon his locality for social relationships, we assume that it has not destroyed this reality for him. Though he may move across community boundaries for work, recreation, worship and education, yet the neighbourhood where he lives—not always easily defined—retains significance for him. There is a practical content of this decision: the community worker is usually involved with a local community with geographical definition that is his commonest work unit, constituency and raw material.

Social relationships

But we would not want to press the first principle to a doctrinaire point. The process and method of community work apply to associations of interests as well as to those of residence—to a college of further education and a hospital, say, as well as to a suburb or the central twilight area of a large city. In fact, our interest in what follows, and the primary goal of community work, is in the social relationships which may develop, rather than in geography or administrative or formal structures. So our first definition is modified and should read—'A community is a social group, usually localized, in which there is manifest or latent, existent or potential, a sense of identification among the members: it is not simply a point on the map but an understanding to be found in people's attitudes and thinking.'

Value judgments

Unlike sociologists, educationists and social workers cannot afford the luxury of being 'value-free'. With many safeguards, that we shall discuss later, they act on the assumption that some things are better for people than other things: in this case, that integrated community action is better than isolation and fragmentation. Without sharing any of the extreme interpretations, this conclusion is based on the view that many aspects of community association and action, which grew naturally in 'the old days', have been seriously inhibited by the conditions of modern living. So in many cases community development can no longer be left to chance but has to be encouraged by organized efforts. This does not mean, for example, that we must paint city life in the darkest hues or conclude that there are no helpful forms of human fellowship there. But it does rest on the view that urbanized living (to restrict ourselves to this one example) is often characterized by segregation, fragmentation, loneliness, anonymity and social problems.

2 What is community development?

Ambiguity in 'community development'

In the last chapter we encountered the many ambiguities in the use of the nouns of this subject and carefully picked our way over the uncertain ground to a place where we could describe our own use of language. Now, moving on, we find ourselves confronted by an equal confusion in the use of the verbs. This means that the terms used to describe a process do not always mean the same thing in different companies, countries, cultures and books. There are in fact at least five descriptions representing a cluster of ideas which overlap and conflict in meaning depending on where they are used and by whom. The five are 'community work', 'community organization', 'community development', 'community education' and 'community relations'. To use the last reference as an immediate illustration: on one side of the Atlantic, in the USA, it is most likely to mean that aspect of the work of a social agency or business organization which involves the encouragement of good public relationships—as they say, 'projecting the right image'.[1] But in Britain the term will probably be understood to refer to organized efforts to help Commonwealth citizens and the host community to understand each other and live together in co-operation and harmony.

In truth, since the movement has become international with a world-wide network, community work requires an agreed international language, a sort of specialized, technical Esperanto. We cannot hope to contribute to this possibility. Our humbler aspiration is that the use of terms describing processes in this book shall be clear.

Usages in Britain and the USA

Some of the major ambiguities lie between the different and converging definitions in the USA and Britain. This has been particularly confusing for countries in the developing regions since in many cases their social workers have been trained either in the USA or in Britain. Now they are often found working together when they have, so to speak, learned different languages. 'Community organization' in the USA is frequently used to describe a process where the emphasis is upon non-directive approaches, the insistence that members of a community shall work through their own problems, decide on solutions and organize their resources, the notion of participation to the fore. The same phrase used in Britain would be more likely to direct attention to the structure of a community, the patterns of power, the relationships of various committees and officials, both statutory and voluntary, all the formal arrangements which lie behind community provision. We should be more likely to use the term 'community development' to describe what our American friends have in mind by 'community organization'.

Usages in developed and developing countries

Another confusion arises by the equal use of 'community development' to apply to the situations both in developing and developed countries. There are of course common areas of application to both circumstances. For example, as we shall see, there is a general understanding that the need for community work arises partly from the effects of social change created mainly by technological change.[2] This applies to Britain no less than to India. But there are so many differences between the two environments that it is not always useful to lump them together. The main intention of community development in a developed country like Britain is to bring the democratic process up to date, refine it, carry it to a logical conclusion on the contemporary scene. The movement in developed countries is primarily about the dignity and the satisfactions of participation. True, there are, even in places like Britain, large pockets of economic need—poverty, poor housing, and the like—and these are more likely to be filled by an integrated use of the community's resources. But in a welfare state, community development is not focused on the need to supply the basic necessities of life to all the citizens—health services, food, clean water supply, primary, secondary and vocational education and work. Now these are precisely the issues with which the process is concerned in the poorer countries. There are areas of the inhabited earth where the overwhelming majority of new-born babies are doomed to a life-span which includes rarely having enough to eat, never receiving any secondary education and suffering chronic unemployment or under-employment during the whole of their adulthood. A proper understanding of their plight realizes that it could be alleviated, if not removed, by an integrated and organized use of limited community resources, and by the encouragement of self-help both in the family and the whole neighbourhood. (In many cases an intense loyalty to one's own kin exists side by side with an indifference to the needs of those outside one's kinship group.) A process of community development here, whilst not blind to the possibility of satisfying social and psychological needs, must aim first at the flow of goods which will meet basic needs.

In 1971 I visited the 'Bangladesh' camp for East Pakistani refugees at Salt Lake City a few miles outside Calcutta. It was a distressing scene. Many children were seriously ill and a number of them were dying. What made matters worse was that for many cases of malnutrition there was, close at hand, a remedy. The international agencies were distributing a powdered protein whose curative effects worked quickly. But the stuff had to be given in the most accurately measured quantities according to the instructions on the printed form which accompanied the packet. Too little and there was no improvement: too much and there was a marked deterioration in the child's condition. Unfortunately, many of the Pakistani mothers were illiterate and could not read the instructions. Self-help processes were required for a practical and urgent result.

The difference between the process in the two locations is not absolute. It can cogently be argued, for example, that a community group can help with many bread-and-butter problems. But the nature of the tasks varies in the contrasted cultures to a degree that can make it unhelpful to use the same description for both.

Community work and political action

Further misunderstandings arise because community developers will be found to have divergent views about the amount of political action which will be involved in their work. At one end of the continuum are those who are prepared to accept society as they find it, more or less, and by programmes and projects of integration, co-operation and education make the existing agencies more efficient in promoting a better quality of life for the citizens. They will initiate change but they do not wish to overthrow: they will complain and rebel, but they avoid confrontation or revolution. By complete contrast are those colleagues in the work who are motivated by the conviction that the system is wrong and must be challenged, broken, replaced: this can only be achieved by sharp confrontations, protesting, demonstrating, undermining the present regime, lobbying and a host of related enterprises. (This second approach, at least in its more extreme form, is often more accurately called 'community action'.) A young full-time community worker, whose constituency is a 'slum' neighbourhood in a large city, recently told me that so far as he knew all the youths he was in touch with were regularly engaged in pilfering from the large shops in the centre. Then he went on: 'But I don't blame them. Our society is so corrupt that it is right to steal from it.' The nature of political commitment is a constant theme for discussion by community workers. Whilst there would be wide agreement that the social worker today may have to go beyond helping the individual client to adjust to his circumstances, and may have to find ways of helping to change those circumstances if they are unjust and depressing, yet no consensus could be reached about the priority of political action—both constitutional and unconstitutional. Significant is the review of the first Gulbenkian report by an American professor.[3]

> The magnitude of the problems in the States has pushed us more in the direction of institutional change. . . . The 'grass roots' approach has moved heavily toward processes of confrontation and conflict to achieve institutional change. . . . It [the Gulbenkian report] may reflect a lack of readiness for a problem-solving focus so essential to successful community work.

Later in this chapter when we offer our own definition it will be seen to take account of the question of political orientation.

The Gulbenkian report adopted a neat device for solving the dilemma. (There were those who thought that it thereby evaded the issue and took the line of least resistance.) It simply used 'community work' as being the more inclusive term. The title is justified by the contents since the text refers to a number of related activities in the one enterprise (p. 149).

> Community work includes: (a) helping local people to decide, plan and take action to meet their own needs with the help of available outside resources: (b) helping local services to become more effective, usable and accessible to those whose needs they are trying to meet: (c) taking account of the interrelation between different services in planning for people: (d) forecasting necessary adaptations to meet new social needs in constantly changing circumstances.

Yet elsewhere the report makes it clear that self-determination by the members of a community is not merely a constituent element of the process but its primary goal: 'the essential purpose of all community work is to enable people to play a more effective part in social affairs' (p. 143).

The weakness of the Gulbenkian definition is that it does not of itself suggest this distinctiveness. It is prone to secure the approval of people who have not grasped the centrality of the notion of self-determination in the modern concept of community work. It may fail to prompt those who say, 'I have been doing community work all my life' to apply this 'new' criterion to their efforts. Perhaps the title was chosen for political reasons, or to facilitate communication and acceptance. In the latter case, there is a sense in which they may have succeeded only too well.

Present use of 'community development'

Our use of the term is close to the Gulbenkian but it insists that we should apply the criterion of self-determination more rigidly to the inclusive processes of community work. Or, to put the matter another way—it has to be recognized that 'community work' is not a process which has been invented in the twentieth century. We can see it present in the efforts of many missionaries overseas during several centuries. In this country it was demonstrated in the past through university settlements, mechanics' institutes, adult education, friendly societies and trade unions—to name but a few examples. Nor is it true to suggest that among those who went before us the stress on self-determination was entirely missing: or that our predecessors were completely paternalistic, determined to do good to others with no offers of decisions about what that 'good' was to be. Canon Bartlett, the founder of Toynbee Hall and an early pioneer, said, 'Little can be done for, which is not with people', and again, 'You are not to do him good, you know.'

Yet in the vastly changed conditions of our time there has to be—for reasons to be examined later—a new emphasis on the active participation even of the deprived citizen in the amelioration of his lot. It has been said that 'we have advanced to the conception of a society that is healthily educative in all its functions'.[4]

Our use of the title 'community development' describes a process which includes three elements: but in giving prominence to the third, we believe that we reflect the best intentions of the movement today.

Community resources for each

The notes of Victorian individualism sound strange in modern ears. Politicians and moral philosophers were usually agreed on the proposition that to give too much support to the individual was to sap his independence and initiative. Every man could look after his own if only he tried hard enough. The sources of neglect were to be found in the family not in the State.[5]

> Booth's work was done at a time when it had come to be assumed by nearly all those in positions of power and influence, including those whose lives were lived with any degree of security or affluence, that every man had a fair chance of making his own way in the world, and caring adequately for his family, if he would work with true diligence, and spend and save responsibly. Those who did not do so were to be blamed for their moral shortcomings: they could not be helped in the mass by making gifts to them in cash or in kind to supplement their earnings, for this would merely lead to the undermining of self-reliance and the exacerbation of poverty, rather than to any improvement in social welfare.

A terse generalization would say that in those days the deprived citizen was thought of as a 'sinner' rather than a 'victim'.

But already in Victorian times we see the powerful beginnings of a new approach in the growth of voluntary organizations and associations, an expression of the strength and support which could be brought to the individual through solidarity. The trade union movement, for example, is one of a number of variations on the theme, 'One man is no man. In unity lies strength.' There were many other forms of association motivated by the conviction that the hard-pressed individual could not simply be left to fend for himself: he needed support from the community.[6]

> All these associations, societies, brotherhoods, alliances,
> institutes and so on, which must be counted by the thousand
> in Europe alone, and each of them which represents an immense
> amount of voluntary, unambitious and unpaid or underpaid
> work, what are they but so many manifestations of the same,
> ever-living tendency of man towards mutual aid and support.

In our day this approach has received widespread support. There is a new climate of opinion about deprivation. Our spontaneous reactions to deprivation are in strongest contrast to Victorian individualism. When we encounter, say, the plight of under-privileged children, we do not say, 'What are his parents doing to allow this to happen?' We are far more likely to think, 'What is our society doing to allow this to happen?' The 'new' attitude represents a change of emphasis even from the beginnings of community work in the last century. For our expectations are far more likely to be directed to the whole society than to active sections: we look for action by statutory agencies through new legislation and State provision rather than from voluntary organizations and associations. The great days of the voluntaryists in education and social work are over, though this is not to deny, of course, that in many areas of provision a useful partnership has developed between statutory and voluntary agencies.

Predictably, and of necessity, another development has emerged —an emphasis upon integrated approaches by the community to the needs of the individual. To appreciate the point one has to recognize that with the growth of State provision there grew up specialized agencies each concerned with one aspect of human need. One department looked after a child if he was unsupported by his family, another if he broke the law. One department was responsible for the provision of better houses, another for the provision of social amenities which might encourage a new housing estate to become a community. The consequences were plain for all to see—overlapping, fragmentation of effort, wastage of resources, helping agencies existing in watertight compartments and approaches which concentrated on one need of the citizen rather than on a human being with many related needs. From these circumstances has arisen the strong demand for an integrated provision. Architects and planners are not just to provide houses and roads: they are creating the environment in which human beings will live. Teachers are not there merely to communicate knowledge: they have to take serious account of the neighbourhood in which their pupils live and require some of the insights of the social worker. The Seebohm Report[7] was decisive in this respect. With the exception of the probation officers, it brought all the different kinds of social workers in a local authority area into one department. Specialization gave way to integration. There are no longer 'child care officers' and 'welfare officers': all are 'social workers': and though their daily duties may still represent a measure of specialization, yet ideally they are working together, in co-operation: integrated approaches to human need are encouraged by the new structures. The 'Seebohm' change has caught our attention to a degree that we may allow it to dominate the picture. We may forget that the integrated approach is intended to include not only those who in the strictest meaning of the word are described as 'social workers' but all those whose daily work affects profoundly the experience of other people. So, as we have seen, architects, planners, doctors and teachers are to be included among those who will want to grasp the total needs of people and work in co-operation with other community providers.

Self-help

There is another notion of community work which is present in nineteenth-century schemes but also receives added emphasis today. This is the idea that people should be encouraged to help themselves rather than be helped. Community provision acquired in the early days a flavour of community education. This is more than a revival of the old individualism which placed the onus on the citizen: it refers to the development of a community's own resources rather than the reliance upon outside support. For though the early efforts were powerfully influenced by ideals of *noblesse oblige,* the conviction that the privileged must share their advantages with those who are not so fortunate and indeed are—heavily —handicapped in the race: and though inevitably this means that the early efforts were tinged with patronage and benevolent despotism, nevertheless it should not be forgotten that many of these pioneering enterprises—like the attempts of F. D. Maurice and Thomas Hughes to establish working-men's colleges—had educational goals and aimed to help the poor to develop their own resources. The importance of self-help in community work has been demonstrated and reinforced by the contemporary examples of community work in poor, developing countries. The point is often expressed in aphorisms like, 'Give a man a fish and you feed him for a day. Teach him to fish and you feed him for life.' Aid from the richer countries seeks to be directed at improving the skills of the indigenous population rather than just the transfer of goods. A raising of agricultural skills in Indian villages, for example, will pay higher dividends than the transfer of a part of American surplus food supplies.

In contemporary Britain, the heavy stress on self-help in community work can be traced to two realities. One is the shortage of all kinds of outside resources for all kinds of human needs. There is just not enough manpower or money to satisfy all the legitimate demands. With limited resources, painful decisions are constantly made about the order of priorities. There is, then, a severely practical consideration behind the insistence that the citizens in a neighbourhood make the maximum use of their own resources. An adventure playground may be possible if the fathers will undertake some of the work. Old people may be better cared for if the efforts of professional social workers are reinforced by the endeavours of an army of voluntary workers. Youth service in this country can only be maintained by the participation of thousands of unpaid enthusiasts. The second reason for the prominence of self-help is the strength of democratic sentiment. 'Doing things for people' at worst denigrates their humanity, denies their dignity and lowers their status. Social interventionists are there to make themselves unnecessary: they fill in a gap until the citizens can realize their own possibilities and gather the self-confidence to exploit them. This topic provides an easy transition to the next session where we suggest that self-determination is the *sine qua non* of community development.

c

Communities decide their own needs

In a definition which promises to become classic, Ross has written:[8]

> stress is laid on the need to encourage communities of people
> to identify their own wants and needs and to work co-
> operatively at satisfying them. Projects are not predetermined
> but develop as discussion in communities is encouraged,
> proceeds and focuses the real concerns of the people. As wants
> and needs are defined and solutions sought, aid may be
> provided by national governments or international organizations.
> But the emphasis is on communities of people working at their
> own problems.

This means that community workers are more interested in a process than in a tangible result and if a choice has to be made they are prepared to affirm that though a project did not reach its stated objective, yet the effort was fully justified on the grounds that the community has learned to take responsibility for itself and use its inner resources. The belief is that they will be better fitted to cope with future problems. Typical of these standards is the report of a small team of the Young Volunteer Force stationed on a housing estate in Stoke. One of the projects was to mount a public demand that an ugly brook area which ran through the estate should be changed into a recreation centre. In the end they succeeded in gaining this objective but their report shows that the test of their endeavours is in the process of community education rather than in persuading the city authorities to pass the plans for the transformation of the brook area.[9]

> It is fair to say that more people have a better knowledge of the
> workings of local government. . . . There is solid achievement
> in terms of the flow of information and growing potential for
> change. . . . This is seen particularly in terms of interest in a
> neighbourhood council and in ensuring that the reclamation
> scheme is followed up.

This is typical of many similar evaluations. The treasure is not the concrete gain, be it adventure playground, traffic-crossing near a school or community centre: it is the intangible and continuing asset of a community which has learned to act in co-operation on its own behalf.

This is so much the case that the literature of the subject provides frequent illustrations of programmes which are criticized because, though they secured desirable changes, they neglected to ensure that those changes were chosen and desired by the members of the community: in other words, community action has not been a result of community education, participation and involvement. For example, Poster writes in high praise of Henry Morris's vision and achievement in the creation of the village colleges.[10] He saw that education was the key to the welfare of rural communities: understood the need to pool the available resources for an integrated approach: appreciated the contribution of architecture to the erection of working buildings. But a major criticism of the scheme, in Poster's view, is that it was imposed upon the people rather than being an expression of their needs.[11]

> Finally the Colleges were the product of benevolent paternalism. They lacked the grass-roots origins of their Danish counterparts, and whatever support they were later to command, largely through used participation in their members' Councils, they did not come into being as part of a significant democratic movement.

Elsewhere in the literature which records the accounts of community projects, plenty of illustrations are provided of how excellent schemes for improvement were frustrated because the organizers failed to take account of the thoughts and wishes of the people. These illustrations are frequently not without humour (as well as being salutary) since they exposed the *naïveté* of intelligent and well-intentioned planners. An agent sought to introduce a new hybrid corn to a small farming community.[12] At a series of meetings he clearly demonstrated its superiority over the traditional type—higher yield and so on. A demonstration plot clearly showed a tripled crop and as a result forty farmers planted the hybrid and each doubled his production in the first year. But the experiment was a dismal failure. Three years after its introduction all but three of the farmers had gone back to the old corn. The explanation was simple. The wives had complained. They did not like the colour or the texture of the new corn. The planners were well informed about the technology of the matter but they had taken little account of social customs. The introduction of 'beneficial' changes by outsiders can be positively harmful for living communities. This has been well understood with respect to the impact of Western technology upon traditional and developing countries and indeed has been, as we shall see, one of the main motives for a community development approach in these regions.[13]

> Emphasis was placed upon the wholeness of the cultural pattern and the disruptive effects of a change which threw one part of the culture out, as when fire-arms led to the disappearance of the buffalo, or the introduction of factory-made cloth destroyed the weaver's handicraft and status, mission teaching upset the authority of the garden magician, or the acceptance of a new religion led to a lop-sided development of black magic, or the introduction of sheep as man's property upset the previous matrilineal ownership of land and agricultural products, or the mission teaching about forbidden decrees of marriage wrecked a social system based on cousin marriage, or the elimination of pagan holidays led to a change in food consumption and so to undernourishment, or the introduction of a head tax necessitated all the young men going away to work.

Elsewhere there are many illustrations, both from Britain and abroad, exhibiting a measure of success, where the object has been to encourage communities themselves to initiate necessary change.[14]

An insistence on self-determination in community work was inevitable and predictable in the light of parallel development in other branches of social work. Professionalism in casework has come to mean the encouragement of the client to work out the solution of his own problems rather than the acceptance of the counsellor's interpretations. Similarly, the group worker seeks to play, not an authoritarian role, but one that will prompt the group to develop its own resources. By a logical progression, these principles are deemed of major importance when the constituency is larger. But in all three areas we find an insistence that self-determination should not be carried to doctrinaire or absurd levels. Individuals, groups and communities are alike in the sense that they are not always capable of defining their needs or of satisfying them when they can, even with outside help. We shall have to consider at a later stage the acceptable rules for the limitation of self-determination. But it ought to be said at this stage that in talking about community development we are referring to an ideal aspiration rather than an ever-present possibility. The right question to ask about community projects is not whether they were '100 per cent pure' from the standpoint of self-determination, but whether the possibilities of self-determination in that particular situation were understood, maximized and used to the full. Had this always been understood we should have been saved many disappointments and much breast-beating: we should have been spared a few of the severest criticisms of community-development projects.

It is the application of the same principle which answers our own dilemma about the degree of political action to be permitted in the definition. Where the worker is primarily concerned to forward a political creed to which he adheres and uses 'community development techniques' to this end—and such operators are not unknown in Britain and elsewhere—then, in the opinion of the present work, this is not community development. This style clearly involves the operator in knowing the answers from the beginning and not allowing them to emerge from the people. But where the operators as loyal instruments of self-determination find themselves confronted by the need for political action, we deem that they are engaged in community development if they go forward. Nay more—they would betray the movement if they refused the challenge. The rubric is demonstrated by the endeavours of a group of Birmingham university students who, a few years ago, were engaged in a piece of community work in a notoriously under-privileged neighbourhood of the city. Their primary purpose was to help the community to develop its own resources to improve the lives of the inhabitants by the enhancement of the total environment. They saw themselves primarily as enablers and their own evaluation at the end of the exercise considers that they have failed, precisely because they have failed to help the community to define and deal with its own problems. But what is interesting is that to attempt their main purpose involved them in different kinds of activities: the encouragement of local committees: acts of personal service for those handicapped by age, disease or circumstance: the supply of information about existing social services: involvement in political campaigns such as campaigns to bring pressure on the city authorities for the swifter repair of publicly-owned property in the neighbourhood. Political action followed the logic of community development: it was not the case that community-development principles were used to support a political aim. Thus the enterprise qualifies for inclusion in the type of activity which we are calling 'community development'.

Summary

In the present work, 'community development' describes a process —usually in neighbourhoods, more rarely in communities of interest—where attempts are made to mobilize the total resources of the community for the protection, support and enrichment of individuals and groups being part of the whole. From this single aim may spring various activities including the integration of social service, the inauguration of *ad hoc* committees and associations, the spread of information about existing provision, acts of personal service and political action. Whenever there is a choice, self-help will be preferred to outside help. The criterion applied to all these efforts will be how far they maximize the possibilities of the community's self-determination: they will be judged to have succeeded or failed by the practical demonstration in all feasible areas, or the hope that the community should define its own needs and organize resources to satisfy them.

3

The work of the community developers

Differences and similarities

There are a few countries in the world where the educational system is rigidly organized. Every school in the land follows precisely the same curriculum for every group at stated periods. It is said that an official in the department of education in each of these countries can say at any one time what is being attempted in every classroom.

The work of community developers in most societies is in strongest contrast to this neat system. If, with the use of strategically placed television cameras, we could have a quick overview of what one hundred of them were doing next Tuesday afternoon, they would be found to be occupied with many differing tasks. And the circumstances of their role would show wide variations. Some would be working at specific tasks like helping immigrant groups to adjust to their new circumstances, whilst others would be working with groups that claimed to be representative of the whole community. Some would be employed by government agencies, whether local or national, whilst others would be on the pay-roll of voluntary organizations. Given the circumstances and the locality they could be found concentrating on the encouragement of political action or the search for volunteers to man an adventure playground. They may have been invited to service a number of existing community groups or they may 'start with nothing' and seek to encourage the formation of community groups. In short, our bird's-eye view would not reveal an impressive uniformity in the actions of community developers, though, as we hope to suggest, there could well be a unity of purpose behind the diversity.

What follows is semi-documentary in that it is composed of brief accounts of the efforts of community developers known to the writer and happening in different parts of the country at the same time.

Frank is a group member of the Young Volunteer Force team at work in a northern industrial city. The education committee which gave the grant that made the work possible thought that he and his colleagues were coming to encourage young people to engage in voluntary service. They were a little surprised to discover that Frank and the others interpreted their role rather differently. Their endeavours were directed to encouraging the local community to be more active on its own behalf. A tenants' association has been formed. They discuss what amenities are required. The ruling political party has been compelled to discuss proposed measures affecting the neighbourhood with the residents. A monthly news-sheet is widely distributed on the estate and seeks to lift the level of active participation in public affairs.

A pretty Warwickshire village comes under the jurisdiction of a nearby town. The inhabitants were dismayed recently to learn that the council had decided to place an incinerator in one of the fields of the village as part of the salvage operations. The inhabitants—who included a number of influential and professional people—were able to mount an impressive campaign against the measure. A large proportion of the small community was involved in being active on its own behalf. Attractive posters were erected: pressure was brought to bear in the right quarter: national publicity was secured in the papers and on radio and television. Eventually, the decision was reversed and the incinerator was sited in another locality, which, incidentally, lacked comparable resources for resistance.

Bill was a councillor who rose very quickly to fame in local politics. He modestly attributed his progress mainly to one factor. He practised 'community politics'. He held a series of public meetings in his ward when he invited people to speak of their needs and problems and discussed with them and explained issues which were to come before the council.

Winifred was employed by the London Council of Social Service to assist the community groups on housing estates, autonomous associations which aimed to improve the amenities and welfare of the people. As requested, she was able to provide several services. Once she was able, behind the scenes, to offer a bit of training to a new secretary. Her presence and interventions at meetings have sometimes helped the group to define their objectives, face their problems, organize their resources and evaluate their work. When two key officials were in sharp conflict she was able to improve the situation by suggesting consultation with a third party who was wise and experienced. She does not see herself maintaining indefinitely the same degree of involvement with the group but hopes progressively to withdraw as they become more self-sufficient.

A chief education officer is dedicated to the encouragement in his authority of 'community colleges'. He means by this not merely educational establishments which cater for all age groups and make different provisions, for example including a library and a youth club: nor does he mean only that courses giving information about the community should be on the curriculum. He looks for members of the community to be involved with the professional educators in the running of the educational establishments. One of his prize exhibits is a swimming pool which was largely provided by local voluntary efforts of the community.

On a large housing estate a demand came from the citizens that they should have their own youth centre. The local vicar became the spokesman for these hopes and he gathered a committee which began to make the required contacts with the education authorities. He also organized a number of 'town's meetings' at which the residents appointed a new committee and discussed specific ideas concerned with the project. At a later meeting the architect brought tentative plans for the centre and discussed with the town's meeting the siting and design of the new building. Several ideas were accepted and incorporated in the final decisions.

Henry Osmond is the local representative and producer for a BBC local radio station which covers a wide area and includes several geographical cultures. He has now been at work for a year and has succeeded in building a relationship with many groups and individuals in this area. More and more people are coming to think of the station as 'theirs', as a channel for the expression of their culture, needs and problems.

A few years ago a large number of undergraduates in a university city decided to contract out of the usual Rag Week celebrations which they judged to be childish. A further objection was that it involved them in collecting for good causes of which they had little personal knowledge. For the old enterprise they substituted a festival week with which was linked a sustained period of community work in a poor district of the city. This involved them in many acts of social work of a personal kind, like undertaking errands for the solitary, old and sick. But they were primarily concerned to discover what were the clamant and neglected needs of the people in the neighbourhood and to encourage indigenous groups to act to meet those needs. So with the help of the medical faculty of the university they conducted a survey to measure the incidence of hypothermia among old people in a hard winter—and found it alarmingly high. They encouraged local action groups to press for speedier attention to house repairs by the corporation landlords.

At first glance we may be struck with the diversities which are represented here, but deeper reflection may disclose a unity both of purpose and method. In at least a part of their operations these people were united. First, their focus of attention, their unit of work, was a community as a whole. They were not primarily concerned with individuals at this time, though their general efforts might involve a fair amount of time being spent in private interviews. Again, they were not fastening their enlarging gaze on small groups, though their primary goal might involve this kind of engagement. But it was a whole community—whether of the geographical or interest nature—which they sought to benefit and whose resources they hoped to mobilize. The other common factor is their claim—however short of it they might fall in practice —that they wanted to encourage a community to use self-help for self-chosen goals.

But equally, of course, the operatives we have described have differences as well as similarities. In fact they illustrate a threefold division of community workers which was first set out in the Gulbenkian report[1] and which is on the way to becoming famous in this universe of discourse.

1   The 'grass roots' worker who operates in a local community usually with groups of people who have come into existence or are being brought to birth in order to effect social change: Winifred, in our list, is one of these.

2   Officials for whom the work of community development is only a part, smaller or larger, of their total duties. So, choosing from our illustrations, we might remind ourselves that the vicar has also the responsibility for the conduct of religious services: teachers are concerned to stimulate the minds and kindle the imaginations of the scholars in their schools as well as to encourage community participation: BBC producers are not without

concern for the technical standards of their programmes and the size of the listening audiences.

3   The chief education officer is a specialized example of a third kind of community worker who is responsible for planning for the lives of a great many people and who may well use a combination of technical and administrative expertise. This category would include planners, architects, politicians and many types of administrative officers. The cogent argument is that such a one needs to be as aware as possible of the total needs of the people for whom he plans: this could result in co-operation with other providing agencies, facilitating an integrated approach to the welfare of the people: it could also imply not always being sure of knowing the precise needs of the people until they themselves have been consulted.

Grass roots community workers

The 'grass roots' community worker exhibits development aspirations in their purest form by his specialism and by his concentration on process rather than product: he is more concerned to identify success in the educational gains by a neighbourhood whose inhabitants have learned to carry more responsibility for their life together, rather than to point to any tangible result of his efforts. As yet, we lack any considerable British case work material of this kind. But we have one work by George Goetschius[2] which is valuable alike for the breadth of its material and for a sustained analysis of the social processes concerned. His raw material was the history of community groups on London housing estates through fifteen years, and he concentrated his attention on the role of the professional social worker who serviced those groups. Far more material is available about comparable efforts on the American scene. A characteristic example is Ross's absorbing account of the adventures of Jack Barnes who was appointed to be first director of recreation in Elmsville, a town of 8,000 people.[3] He found no welcome awaiting him and no expectations about the work he was to do. His appointment was a compromise solution between conflicting pressure groups: the main object seems to have been to use up the funds of a trust before all the trustees died. However, he gained wider acceptance by the successful establishment of four playgrounds with regular programmes during the day and in the evening. But at the centre of approval and congratulations, Barnes was not satisfied with himself.[4]

> He did not consider himself a playground director, or a recreational leader, or a teacher of swimming. These things he did as a way of both rendering a useful service and beginning a larger job. This larger task he saw as helping the community of Elmsville develop ability to pull itself out of its apathy and to do something as a community to improve itself.

The remainder of the account is instructive for those who wish to understand the community-development process. It relates how Barnes set out to understand Elmsville better, to identify, for example, what sub-groups made up the whole. He persuaded them to set up a community council. Out of growing respect for him the first meeting was well attended, but he was shocked by their apathy and disappointed by their unwillingness to focus on specific issues like the lack of garbage collection and the absence of a library. Soon afterwards the complacency of Elmsville was shattered by the adverse criticism of a few distinguished visitors who described the town as 'decayed and dying', 'unaffected by the trends of modern life and indifferent to its responsibilities and opportunities'. Barnes now found himself at the centre of expectations so that he could organize the desires of the citizens of Elmsville to change their way of life. He arranged a visit by the council to a town of comparable size with a reputation as a progressive community. This experience proved a powerful stimulant. Plans were approved for programmes and projects in each area of need defined by the people's council. Goals were recognized and duties accepted by the citizens themselves. When, after three years, Barnes left to take up another appointment, the local judge who made the formal speech of farewell said:[5]

> We feel that *we* ourselves have got the library, that *we* run the P.T.A., that *we* started and still operate the community concern series, that committees run the children and youth programs, that *we* got the garbage collection in this city, that *we* changed the traffic regulations, and so on. Barnes didn't do those things: *we* did. And here is the secret, I believe,

of his work and effectiveness here. He was able to get *us* to be aware of what was going on, he got *us* interested, he got *us* doing things. And now that he is going, the greatest tribute to his work is that he can go knowing that we realize our responsibilities and that we'll carry on.

From this single typical instance emerges a number of principles which relate to the processes and objectives of the community worker in many contrasted settings. Barnes is more concerned with the growth of community responsibility, widely spread and shared, than with the attainment of concrete objectives in which he, perhaps along with an élitist minority, has played an exclusive or even dominating role. He wants to encourage in Elmsville the use of social processes to achieve self-chosen goals and objectives. He sees himself with a limited time space, working to make himself unnecessary. Had the work collapsed on his departure he would have judged himself to be a failure, for his primary objective is to help the community itself to accept responsibility and achieve status, which involves working at its own pace and in its own way.

Within those broad limits there will be variations in the circumstances and to some extent the methods of community workers. Elmsville must not be seen as the prototype for similar enterprises anywhere in the world! For example, the grass roots worker may go to a neighbourhood where there are already in existence autonomous community groups: he might see his main function as being to strengthen these and work to co-ordinate their efforts. By contrast, like Barnes, he may find himself in a place where there are virtually no such groups with any significance for the whole area and he could then decide that his first task is to prompt the initiation of such groups. Another difference relates to the circumstances of his own appointment. Is he the employee of a voluntary organization? Or has he been hired by a statutory authority, whether local or national? Or after the peculiarly British fashion, are the conditions of his appointment a mixture of both these elements? The employing agency has important consequences for the worker in terms of support, sanctions and role-identity. In Britain we usually find him working with groups rather than the whole neighbourhood. Very often he is seen to have a specific task such as the common example of encouraging harmony and co-operation between members of different ethnic groups, or between 'the host community and immigrants'.

However, despite these wide variations, there are common features of grass roots community workers whether they function in Toronto or Timbuktu. In focusing on the community and working with non-directive approaches they recognize that there are shared goals as the tangible evidence that participation and responsibility are producing a better quality of life for the citizens. These could be said to be:

Amenities—like the provision of an adventure playground. Educational schemes of all types and for all ages come under this heading.

Welfare—like ensuring that the poor, lonely, ill, handicapped and old receive the support they need.

Working out conflict—like trying to ensure that groups with different attitudes learn to respect each other and find the cause of integrated action.

Representation to controlling authorities—like organizing a deputation to the housing department of the local authority to discuss a grievance about the implementations of the regulations.

Co-operation—whatever the outcome, it is believed that co-operation is better than fragmentation since it encourages community feeling and social relationships.

Likewise there are universal features of specific processes which local operatives wish to encourage. These might be said to be:

Defining the needs of their own area—for these may not always be what 'outsiders' suppose them to be. A lot of planning has been undertaken on the serene assumption that the planners knew what the citizens needed without bothering to ask them. A committee which is congratulating itself on the acquisition of a children's playground may not realize that the people are more concerned about the noise of the dust chutes.

Deciding priorities. The provision of amenities and welfare services is limited by the scarcity of available resources. Even schemes which require no large expenditure and have a high dependence on voluntary help may find they are short of people. Few associations can attempt all they would like. Priorities should rest on decisions not drifting.

Decisions for action on the basis of needs and priorities. The apostles of change have to deal with mechanisms as well as ideas. There are immediate tasks as well as distant goals. Work groups or committees are formed, meetings arranged, campaigns planned and roles allocated. The consequences of decisions must be faced in individual and corporate responsibility.

Evaluation. The assessment of efforts can be the most important part of the operation. Only by accepting the realities of failure (or partial success) and analysing them can the enterprise go forward and the participants be saved from complacency or despair.

Re-planning. If the analysis of failure or partial success is valid, then something has been learned without too much discouragement and the participants will want to undertake the same or similar enterprise having benefited by previous experience.

Finally, we may say that wherever they may be, grass roots community workers are likely to be found employing one or more of the same five constituent elements of their role. These are:

Supplying information as required. This can include communication about groups who have faced similar problems and literature on the subject and helping agencies both statutory and voluntary. He points to resources. Giving encouragement to groups and individuals in the face of set-back and disappointment.

The minimum intervention which is required to help the association to face the logic of its task, decisions and action.

Liaison officer. The worker acts as a go-between for the sections of the community and the sections of those who are committed to the enterprise. As necessity arises he interprets each to the other, ensures that the communication system is efficient and encourages co-operation.

Teaching organizational and social skills to the people concerned.

Summary

We see the grass roots community worker giving high priority to the development process and concentrating his efforts on helping the people of a locality to use appropriate resources for the enhancement of their life together. The efforts are directed to concrete goals—amenities, welfare, education, entertainment, justice—but ideally he is more concerned with the growth of effective relationships and the habit of co-operative effort.

Implications for other roles

Community development is only one method of social and educational work. Enthusiasts for this approach, concerned to further their cause, would be wise to show themselves aware of this reality. There are those in both spheres who are concerned first of all to give a service to the individual as in the case of the counselling services of the social worker. A teacher too is concerned to stimulate the minds and kindle the imaginations of his pupils as well as to help them to relate to the neighbourhood where they live and the society of which they are citizens. For some of these role-occupants community work is only a secondary function. He would be a poor general practitioner whose diagnostic and healing skill deteriorated on account of his concentration on the community aspects of medicine. Even when there is a clear community aspect of the role, it is often suitably interpreted as being concerned with provision rather than with development. That, in fact, is what is usually intended by the appointment of community officers to the social services departments of local authorities. They are seen to be mainly employed in gaining something for the people and not very much in helping people to gain something for themselves.

But a promising discussion has arisen in Britain and elsewhere. It has two parts. The first asks whether there should not also be a community orientation about the efforts of many role-occupants whom we have previously seen as being almost exclusively concerned with the single, and sometimes the isolated, individual client. The secondary query is whether there are not unexplored examples of where this necessity (to see and understand the client in his social setting) does not present significant opportunities with the process of development as well as provision. Nobody wants to impose a blueprint on all social and educational enterprise. But it could be useful to assess our philosophy, policy and programmes in the light of the changing conditions of our time. It is arguable that in aggregate more hope for an active, participant society rises from the efforts of the people who are peripherally involved than from the professional grass roots operatives who will probably remain in relatively small numbers.

The best-known example is from social work. For a long time the major preoccupation was with casework skills and training courses were geared to this end. The image of the social worker was mainly of one who would be involved with one other person in the interview situation. Moreover, whilst respecting the established course of acceptance and self-determination, his function was to help the client to adjust to his social and economic circumstances—not to try to change them. A first step was taken when it was more comprehensively realized that the client might not be understood or helped apart from the smaller affiliations, like the family, to which he belonged: and group-work skill began to take its place alongside casework on the curricula of training courses. A further, fuller realization held twin aspects. One was the realization that it might not be possible to understand or help a client without taking into account the effect of the neighbourhood and society in which he lived. That could be the source of problem and inadequacy. The second aspect followed logically. There would be cases in which if the social worker was to be true to his vocation, he would work to change the social environment. Thus in two senses the social worker became the community worker. Statements that at the point of contact with the client, he is always a social worker and never a social reformer, are not today greeted with the same unbroken acclaim that was common a few decades ago.

There are many other examples of professions where the notion of 'community' with these twofold implications is beginning to penetrate. The responses vary widely. In some professions, the notion is the enthusiasm of a few whilst the majority are characterized by opposition or lukewarm assent. Among the relevant occupations there are those who are almost exclusively absorbed by the first set of ideas and are concerned only with provision and welfare, whilst others adopt a more radical stance and look to the new approaches to affect profoundly the nature of society itself. Another variable is the continuing prominence given to the specific and specialized service given by these role-incumbents and how far the role-expectations may become diffuse in terms of their contribution to community concerns. There is much confusion but from our perspective we may observe that it is creative

D

confusion. The angel has descended and troubled the waters. Many old-established professions are being re-examined and reassessed by those within the structure. And the measuring rod in their hands records the balance of technical expertise and community involvement and the balance between those two in effective performance. The present state is indeed best described as 'creative confusion': much is not clear but there are signs and a promise of more relevant performance as a result of the conversations that are taking place. The trainers in widely diverse professions are asking what part an understanding of community should play in their courses and how prominently it should loom in the professional duties of their people.

Thus the trainers of doctors, district nurses and policemen are asking these questions. The last is an interesting example. We have become accustomed to thinking of the police force as an authoritarian organization with a rigid hierarchy of leadership and the policeman having the simple duty of law enforcement. But now there is creeping in the notion that he is also a community worker. This is symbolized partly by the appointment of high-ranking officers in local forces to be solely concerned with community relationships, but perhaps even more by new elements in training courses for recruits which reflect the conviction that the policeman is something more than a law enforcement officer: he is also a community worker. 'The Police Service must respond to changes in society and must possess some understanding of the different groups that make up the community.'[6] We are growing accustomed to the spectacle of police cadets working in youth clubs in poor neighbourhoods and joining with others of their own age group in schemes of voluntary service.

Another instructive example is found in the realm of local radio. The original plans of the BBC were for forty stations, but for various reasons this has been cut to twenty. Documents behind the innovation, including the government White Paper, made it clear that these instruments of mass communication were to have distinctive features. Briefly, this amounts to saying that the local enterprise was to be a community station. But during the operational phase a valuable controversy arose about the meaning of this concept. Granted that the goal enclosed agreed elements of providing information, entertainment, education and services of a localized nature, was the aim also to help the people of the area to become active on their own behalf? Was the ultimate distant goal that the station should be run by the citizens with the technical assistance of the professionals? Or was it only that the professionals should produce programmes which they thought were suited to local needs? And if the former was the given answer, does it not appear that there is a gap in the training of the professional producer and programme organizer, since they are fashioned as communicators rather than community educators?

As we have already suggested, the same considerations have been seen to have implications for the training schemes for a wide variety of roles in our society, including civil servants, architects and planners, clergy and members of the legal profession. But we propose to devote longer and special attention to one profession—that of teaching—since there appear to be peculiar issues and opportunities here. One reason is that the concern of teachers with personal development makes this a fitting subject for their concern. Another is the size of the force: over a quarter of a million teachers in this country constitute a considerable potential.

Teachers as community workers

Discussions with many teachers have taught me to tread delicately in urging a consideration of the community work aspect of their role. They are under pressure from many directions today and not uncommonly they are placed at the receiving end of much of the restlessness and lawlessness of our time. Like other educational agencies they are frequently cast for the part of scapegoat. If things are wrong, it is felt, the schools must be to blame: they should also be among the main agents of reform and renewal. Little account may be taken of the fact that the causes of the trouble may well lie beyond the control of the school system: and that they can be cut off even from a feasible contribution by shortage of resources. It has been pointed out by Bryan Wilson that at a time when roles are becoming more specialized, that of the teacher is growing more diffuse.[7] Mays says this ought to be and sees the teacher with more and more of the functions of the social worker.[8] A demand that they should see themselves making a contribution to community feeling is part of a general pattern.

The indications are that many teachers do not interpret their role in this way: they see themselves as having a function which is largely contained within the premises and the activities of the school: they focus on the sharing of knowledge and values and the personal development of their pupils. Mays found no strong inclination among teachers to assume the new role he advocated,[9] and Rudd and Wiseman report that the extension of duties beyond classroom teaching is a major source of grievance.[10] An enquiry in Glasgow a few years ago confirmed most of these findings. 'In many cases the teacher's knowledge of social agencies was slight. . . . Most teachers did not consider it their allocated role to contact agencies.'[11] Musgrove and Taylor too found[12] that teachers did not, for example, welcome parents as active partners helping to make decisions: but they need not have worried, since parents were found to share the teacher's view that education is mainly about the acquisition of knowledge.

It is perhaps instructive to note that, according to Bracey,[13] in the USA the expectations of parents and teachers are far otherwise, at least in small-town communities. Parents play a more active part in the education of their children.

For our educationalists a number of discussion points are raised by a contemplation of the elements of community orientation in schooling.

One is that it raises fundamental questions about the rationale of education. Can its purposes be restricted to the acquisition of knowledge, the encouragement of personal development and socialization to the society's existing norms? Is education primarily about social mobility? Many would say no to these interpretations. Admittedly the concept of community arraigns many present definitions of the purpose of education as incomplete. Do they aim to set human beings free or to produce a new generation of routinees? How far do they take account of W. E. Hocking's much-quoted dictum[14] that the educational purpose is to communicate the type and provide for growth beyond the type?

A related and fruitful controversy compares and contrasts the approaches and methods of teachers and social workers. Despite recent attempts to prove the contrary, they are not the same. The 'client' is thought of in a fundamentally different way in each sphere. In one, he is there partly to receive a body of knowledge and in the other to work out his own problems in a non-directive atmosphere. Practically, here is an argument not for persuading teachers to be social workers, however great the need; perhaps we ought to place professional social workers in schools as auxiliaries to supplement the efforts of teachers. But though there is contrast between the two roles in method and approach, there is also considerable overlap. On the one hand community development is emphatically an educational process since it focuses upon the changes in people's lives and the development of skills to cope with the problems that threaten the common good. On the other hand the educational endeavour has a better chance of success if it takes into account some of the factors that would be important to a community developer as social worker. According to Margaret Mead educationalists are prone to an 'over-evaluation of the educational process, and the under-evaluation of the iron strength of the cultural walls within which any individual can operate'.[15]

In fact, for more than a generation, impressive lip-service has been paid to those ideas by a succession of officially inspired reports on the educational state of the nation. As long ago as 1938 the Spens Report on secondary education was pleading for a definition of the school which saw it as a place where teachers and taught share a common life and are connecting and co-operating parties. The recent Halsey Report[16] on educational priority areas contains an up-dated version of the same theme. Though these ideas may not be taken seriously in practice, they still express a widespread conviction that the school is a social unit within the wider society and that it has become isolated. The need was always there, it is felt, for the school to play a community role but it has become more necessary at a time of rapid social change. In quieter times and more stable days, not only were there more integrating forces at work in human societies, but the school was more likely to be a natural aspect of the community, contributing spontaneously to community feeling. Today, it is argued, the need is greater and the school has to play a more self-conscious and organized part.

Our best hope is for a continuing exchange of ideas and experiences between teachers and community developers. The latter should tread delicately, eschew all suggestions of fanaticism and show themselves sensitive to other aspects of the role of the teachers. They in turn can demonstrate an openness to ideas which surely ought to be part of their professionalism. It can be a fruitful discussion.

In practice, teachers who are 'keen on the community approach' are often found to be working with only a part of the idea or even a distorted version. On a theological analogy, they are heretics rather than unbelievers. For example, in some schools where community studies are being taken up with enthusiasm, they proved on closer scrutiny to be a 'ROSLA' device, that is a positive way of engaging the attention and controlling the behaviour of less intelligent youngsters who have to stay at school for a further reluctant year. It is a sort of poor man's sixth form. One enthusiastic young teacher, obviously doing valuable work in this area, said to me recently, 'My girls cannot be described as "not brainy but good with their hands". So far they have proved not to be good at anything.' In these circumstances the other teachers on the staff are grateful that somebody will take the educational drop-outs off their hands to leave them free to concentrate on the scholars with more promise: in this way they display an indirect enthusiasm for the 'community school'.

Joint discussions on the whole notion are required and a thorough investigation of the implications of this approach for the style of schooling and the functions of the teacher. One young volunteer force developed a programme of community education for the older school children in their area. The heads and their staff were willing to co-operate until they discovered that the scheme involved the youngsters not merely in learning more about their neighbourhood and possibly giving voluntary service to it, but also in looking at its provisions critically. The precise function of community schools is open to widely contrasted interpretations. Gillett[17] has provided a fourfold classification which is by no means exhaustive. The term 'community school' may be thought to apply to any of the following categories:

a   Those which contain all the children in an area.
b   Those where the buildings are frequently open to a variety of groups of adults.
c   Those which make use of the community in their curriculum.
d   Those who set out to serve the community in addition to the community serving them.

One hopes the stage is now set to present proposals for the contribution from community developers to a continuing conversation with teachers. To this end we draw a picture of the 'ideal type' of community school representing a constellation of five ideas. Though this school will nowhere exist, its definition may help the conversation along and even disclose a few possibilities in particular areas.

a   A community school seeks to take account of the impact of the social environment, and particularly the neighbourhood, upon the educational prospects of the child: and where there is deprivation, it wants to redress the balance, say by positive discrimination in favour of the deprived. For education is not of itself the Great Leveller—the dice are loaded against many children before they come to school.

b   It aims to help the youngster come to terms with his community. Ideally this communicates knowledge of the way it works and has implications for the curriculum. It also aims to help each youngster to find his proper place in the community with appropriate elements of acceptance and rejection, belonging and alienation, dependence and service, and hence has implications for programmes of social education.

c   It wants to use the resources of the community in the school seeing the educational process as not restricted to a building or a group of professional teachers, but calling for the involvement of citizens, both parents and others, and the agencies and institutions outside the school. This implies a spread of power.

d   It hopes to serve the community. One way is the use of its premises outside the normal hours of working by groups of all ages. Another is the increasing volume of voluntary service undertaken by scholars.

e   Most idealistically of all, the community school hopes to become an agent for necessary change in the community, not shrinking from the most radical measures if they are justified on the grounds of compassion and justice. Scholars are prepared to participate in social change and even to initiate it when required to do so by circumstances.

The fulfilment of those wild hopes is partly in the hands of the teachers themselves: for they have some freedom to interpret their roles. But much, of course, will depend on the policy of the school and its head and also on the outlook of the authority for which they work.

However, the college of education is the place of beginning if we want teachers to grasp the community-development possibilities which may be implicit in their office. There the student can become familiar with the ideas though it would be unrealistic to expect him to acquire many of the skills. However, this is a subject which belongs more fittingly to the next chapter.

The skill and training of the community worker

Once again, for the sake of clarity, we describe the sense in which several words and concepts are used in this chapter. In talking about skills and training we are entering an arena where professionals in this subject have been engaged for some years in a continuing controversy. We shall not take sides or attempt to pronounce on these issues but the reader has a right to know at least what are the tentative assumptions of the present perspective.

Types of community worker

It has, for example, already been pointed out that there are at least three types of community workers, each demonstrating a distinctive approach and therefore calling for some differentials in skills and perhaps in training.

a   Direct work with local people. This is community development, concerned with informal groups whose needs are not met through the normal channels and where the main objective, using indigenous leaders, is to prompt the local people to accept responsibility for themselves.

b   Agency and inter-agency co-ordination. This is community organization where the object is to work through established agencies, improving their service by integration of effort and the co-operation which diminishes overlapping and the fragmentation of efforts.

c   The work of planners in making provision for sections of the population and who are required in analysis and forecasting to take account of the total needs of people in community.

Now it is true that we have here three identifiably different roles but there are considerable areas of overlap which may perhaps be best interpreted in the light of a shared approach, namely the use of the non-directive method wherever it is possible. In each case these operatives are concerned to work with people as well as for them. There is at least an aspect of their work where they do not approach the 'client' knowing what is good for him but want to facilitate a process by which the 'client' defines his own

45

needs. Of course, the proportion of the non-directive approach will vary in each of the three areas. For the grass roots worker it is dominating, filling the whole of the picture. For the planners it will be less prominent, but even here any major changes are likely to be put out for public discussion before final decisions are made. It is common practice now for the 'green paper' (a document for discussion prior to final decision) to precede the 'white paper'.

In another way, too, scrutiny of the fieldwork reveals considerable areas of overlap between different types of community workers and also between the operations of community workers and other social workers. The grass roots community worker may concentrate his attention and direct his efforts towards the community's own efforts to achieve self-chosen goals. But in practice he will find that he has to respond to other needs not obviously connected with the primary aim. One such worker excused his early withdrawal from a supervisory session by telling me that he had to return to headquarters because an old man would be waiting to take two hours to talk over his personal problems. 'That', he said ruefully, 'is what community development work proves to be in practice.' Frequent dilemmas of this nature arise. If the local people want to use him primarily as personal adviser, counsellor, resource person or provider, he has to be careful how he rejects those roles lest he sacrifice rapport for a doctrinaire insistence on his own role-definition. Conversely, he will not want to be fashioned by the expectations of others to the point where he forfeits his primary purpose. The dilemma which appears in many reports of 'grass roots' projects can be a promising conflict, for community development is an aspiration rather than a panacea. The worker is concerned not only with his ideal intentions but with the art of the possible and inevitable compromises. He is in a sailing boat which must tack and adjust to the wind rather than in a motor boat which is less governed by external conditions.

The implications of this discussion for present purposes are that in thinking of the skill and training community workers require, we cannot put different kinds in separate boxes, so to speak. There is too much overlap for that to be a profitable exercise. So in what follows we are thinking of the skills and training needed by those who would be covered by the generic term 'community worker', though we are assuming that they would be searching for and maximizing the community development elements. At the risk of being tiresomely repetitious, we say again that this refers to a community's use of its own resources for self-chosen goals. In other words, we are expecting that community workers of whatever brand will want to make non-directive approaches to the limit of feasibility.

One other point should be made clear. In previous chapters we have laboured to describe the distinctiveness of the 'community-development process' as it is to be understood in the present work. We understood it to be not the same as provision or organization but a deliberate intention to encourage the members of a community to accept more responsibility for themselves in planning, decision-making and use of resources. The distinction having, as we hope, now been made clear we propose henceforth to use the more general terms 'community work' and 'community workers'. This usage may be justified on the grounds of the considerable overlap in philosophy and practice. ('Community developer', anyway, may suggest links with group photography.)

Role and function of the community worker

In thinking of appropriate skills and training we must not lose sight of those role-incumbents, like teachers and clergy, where community work is only part of what they have to do. If we draw up a list of what is ideally required we must quickly go on to ask how much of this is feasible for people who have to undertake other professional training and duties.

At present there are twin temptations. One is simply to add training for community work to an already heavy programme of professional training until the student is impossibly overloaded. I was once taken to task at a conference because I had to admit under close questioning that we did not include 'Chinese civilization' in a course of training for full-time youth leaders. In reply, I conceded the importance of the subject but pleaded that in a crowded two-year programme it rated low on our list of priorities.

The other temptation is to allow the new role to swamp the old. Liberal and progressive churchmen, for example, may argue that the clergy will be more relevant in modern times if they spend less time conducting ritualistic services, preaching, hearing confessions and more time on community work. Consistently, they require that theological training devotes less time to the study of doctrine, the original language of the Scriptures and church history.

On the present view neither of these solutions is satisfactory. So another approach is suggested. Having drawn up a list of the skills and training required by the community worker, we have to ask, in the case of each of the role-incumbents we have in mind, how much of this is possible in their professional training. As much as possible may be integrated with their general service. One useful arrangement may be to think of the training in community work being offered on two levels. One is a lesser commitment to what would largely be an information-giving course. The other would be a bigger commitment, offered as an option to those who wanted to specialize in this aspect of their role.

Let us make a specific application of these suggestions to school teachers. How far can we expect colleges of education to prepare students to be aware of, and where desired fulfil, the community-work aspect of their role? Their present performance here represents a confused picture. Some have assiduously cultivated this side of the business, others remain blissfully unaware of the new challenges. What makes overall assessment difficult is that it is often impossible to know what is happening and to construct comparative categories because many strangers gather under the umbrella of courses described as 'community studies' in the curricula offered by colleges of education. There are also wide variations in the amount of practical work that is involved.

A reasonable expectation, then, might be that the provision should operate on two levels. Under this scheme the first aim is that every student during his time in college will have the opportunity to appreciate the best intentions of community work, both by study and personal contact. This would be largely an enterprise of information-giving and understanding and would make no pretence to teach the appropriate skills. But there could be more for students who wanted to prepare themselves to be sensitive to the community-work opportunities in their teaching careers. Here a requirement would be not merely longer studies of the background issues but also an arrangement whereby some of their 'practice' time was spent not in schools but in community-work agencies. Personal involvement in community-work processes would be essential for this second course, the whole of which could be an optional extra much as, in many colleges of education now, there are additional courses in youth leadership for those who want to undertake them. The link with their general course could be provided through their main subject which would normally be sociology, but this could be taught from a community standpoint. For a subject which often strikes the student as at once diffuse and remote—partly because it has so many aspects—this is not as unacademic as it may sound. 'Community' thereby becomes a window through which one can look out on the whole sociological landscape—norms, culture, role-relationship, stratification, social control—everything. It can be a perspective that lends coherence to the whole academic subject. More than that it is the background knowledge and understanding which the teacher/community educator needs.

Skills of the community worker

Perfectionism will mock the efforts of an attempt to describe the competence of the community worker. He would be a very remarkable person who combined within himself the qualities and abilities we are about to describe. Nor would all of them be required in equal proportions in every single local circumstance, though all might be required to a degree and a serious deficiency in any area could have disastrous consequences. In any case we are concerned to provide here as full a list as possible, though what follows suggests 'the ideal type' who nowhere exists but whose delineation is not thereby without usefulness.

Analysis

This is a dignified title for the ability to assess and interpret, by more than guess work, what is happening in different human situations and with individuals, groups and communities.

a *Individuals* All behaviour has a reason but we are not always aware of the reasons and it is not cynical to say that often our conscious motives are worthier and more respectable than our unconscious motives. The community worker is brought into touch with many individuals, and with not a few he is required to develop a good and enduring personal relationship. This can be facilitated by an insight into the common motivations of human behaviour.[1]

b *Groups* Our behaviour is affected by the presence of others. This can be most emphatic in small working parties or in committee work in which the community worker will frequently be involved. So he needs to have understanding of the dynamics of the group.[2]

c *Communities* Two features are intended here. One is that there are a few fairly universal structures and processes which can be found in communities. There are always, for example, approved systems and institutions for education and mechanisms of socialization. We can observe the universal element at once if we consider Warren's definition of a community as 'that continuation of social units and systems which perform the major social functions having locality reference'.[3] It is a general definition with a wide application. On the other hand, our worker is concerned with a community no less unique than his own fingerprints. Its particularities will be partly created and partly expressed by a collection of realities which include local trades, personalities, traditions, buildings and location. He has to demonstrate an ability to grasp, not merely community structures and processes in general, but the structures and processes of the town or neighbourhood of the project. His task may not be made easier by the simple fact that he is a stranger who has come from outside and maybe only those who have been born and brought up there can appreciate the subtle nuances of the place. His analytical and interpretive skill and intention will use several methods as appropriate. Simply living in the place may help: listening to many counsellors is another source of local wisdom: walking round the area and acquiring a 'feel' of the neighbourhood is a technique not always to be despised. He needs also access to hard information and he may have to conduct surveys to acquire the evidence on which to found judgments.

One can often test people's awareness of community structures and processes at quite unsophisticated levels because they will describe local realities of which others, long resident in the place, will show themselves blissfully unconscious. 'One of the features of our town of course is that we have three social groups. The older families whose forebears go back to the time when the place was a village. The commuters who work in London but live here: some of them see it primarily as a dormitory suburb. And then there are the people who live on the housing estate and mostly earn their living in the local factory.'

'I suppose I have always known that was true but I have never heard it put into words before.'

'Well, I think we can also see how it works out in practice. People sometimes belong to community groups which express their membership in one of the three social groups. Moreover, whenever we want to do anything together as a community, we have to take this threefold division into account. It can impede full co-operation.'

Admittedly, though semi-documentary, it is undoubtedly an unsophisticated example, though in this world it is the obvious which is frequently overlooked. But more than this will commonly be required from the community worker.

There is also another area no less pertinent for the exercise of his analytical power: and that is in evaluating the various projects in which he is concerned. Those who have shared in the work may not be accustomed or trained to an exercise in which they try to judge objectively a project in which they have been personally involved. They may lack any standards of measurement. Or there may be emotional barriers. An admission even of partial failure may undermine their self-confidence. They may lack the assurance to be satisfied that the enterprise has been worthwhile, though not all their hopes have been fulfilled. Realistic assessment encounters many inhibitions, yet it is important if the project is to contribute to a learning process that may well be more important than any tangible result. Obviously the worker must not only himself have the ability to evaluate what has happened but to facilitate the process by which his colleagues join in the process of assessment.

Communication

A popular misgiving today has passed into a phrase of everyday usage—'there has been a failure in communication'. What rarely happens is that any serious thought is given to the meaning of this judgment. Certainly the community worker cannot be content to leave it there because in diverse ways he is constantly concerned with the matter. He is brought into touch with communication networks which he must understand and to some extent use. He himself has to learn how to communicate effectively with all sorts and conditions of men and groups.

In a large subject we can briefly indicate three relevant areas.

a   Communication is about values as well as facts. Effective systems ensure that participants not only receive the information they require but have an opportunity of discussing the aims and goals of the enterprises in which they are concerned.

b   Efficient communication gives attention to the means which are appropriate to the occasion. Thus there is some material which can be sent through the post but other matters for communication may require a personal encounter. To choose a *reductio ad absurdum*—a written communication may be adequate to ask a member to a committee meeting but not to criticize the part he is playing in the work. Obvious as the point is, much misunderstanding, conflict and wastage arises from the actions of leaders who choose the inappropriate forms of communication.

c   According to Sprott,[4] there are specific criteria which can be applied to communication systems within any type of organization:

    i   Is it two-way? Is there a play-back from the people receiving the facts and values, or do they merely come down from above?

    ii Is it complete? Or are there missing links in the chain? Can anybody say about a vital piece of information, 'But nobody told me'?

    iii Is it intelligible to the recipients? Is it couched in the language and the thought-forms that they can understand?

    iv Is it punctual? Or are the answers to participants' needs and questions long delayed?

    v   Is it fairly flexible? Or is it so rigid that it cannot take account of special circumstances?

Encouragement

As the list grows longer it is clear that we are drawing a picture of a leader who is both task-related and person-orientated, and both in response to the demands of his office. He has to be a person who does not easily lose sight of the goal and who will not become so emotionally involved with the people concerned that he can no longer offer them a professional service or view their situations with objectivity. Again and again he may have to perform for them a 'truth-function', that is bring them back to face the consequences of their needs and decisions. Yet equally he must again and again perform for them a 'love-function'—at least this proves to be the case in practice whatever be the theories of some. And this not only because of the respect and regard which he comes to have for them as fellow human beings, but for the more mundane reason that the hope of successful achievement in community work is thereby enhanced. (I was interested in the casual remark of a young 'grass roots' community worker at the end of our two-hour supervisory session. Through two years he has encountered many setbacks and disappointments. Now the work is showing unmistakable signs of progress. He said, 'I've come to like and respect the people in the neighbourhood.' In my view, he was more, not less, professional because he could make that remark.) Local people are often found to be greatly in need of encouragement. In their work they are often forced into unaccustomed responsibility and prominence. They are easily dashed and their own feelings of inadequacy can be reinforced by relatively minor setbacks. Again and again the community worker is impressed into service as encourager. This is not paternalism but common sense and arises from the situation. And part of this skill is the ability to make and maintain good personal relationships with different kinds of people. Often he has to be able to begin this process early, in other words, to make quick social contact.

Organization

Perhaps it would be nice if our worker could spend nearly all his time listening and talking to individuals and groups. But in actual practice his work load can include a large amount of time spent on administrative chores—secretarial work with and for groups, including minutes, records, accountancy, fund-raising, negotiations with statutory bodies, writing letters and so on. Indeed, one report which investigated thirty projects, saw office work as second in the list of activities which took up most of the worker's time and 'organization' was recorded as one of the skills

E

in which they most needed further training. Perhaps 'chores' is the last word we should have used in this connection. For the art of good organization is simply attention to detail, which is a means of anticipating situations in which people will be able to participate to the limit of their ability. Good organization amongst other things is a way in which we care for people. Efficiency is not the opposite of affection but one of its expressions. This is not a theoretical matter. I have known one or two community workers who would score high marks under the last section of encouragement, but their organization was so slack that it often inhibited their friendliness. They forgot to write the promised letter and misplaced documents or were late for appointments or never produced their copy for the community newspaper on time. The results were that others suffered inconvenience, frustration and loss and the total effort was weakened.

Mediation

The community worker is frequently involved in conflict situations and concerned with others in problem solving. He often finds himself the middleman between two contending parties. This can be when with others he is representing the whole neighbourhood against an outside agency. A fight against the decisions of a department of a local authority or the way which they interpret their regulations is only one example. But equally conflict can arise among the various sections of the neighbourhood and indeed among the community groups themselves. The opening of a recreation room in a hall may be the prelude to a struggle between different groups for its use. Of course the worker wants the parties concerned to work these things out for themselves but he may be called upon to play a more active part in the proceedings than ideally he would like. In any case, however small his own part may be, he wants to judge the situations and choose the most hopeful approaches. The skill of mediation is quite distinctive. It calls for strength and patience, an exquisite sense of timing and the insight to choose the right forms of intervention. Conflict can be promising and productive if it is worked through by people who face the issue involved and will not allow themselves to be diverted by the emotional content of the difference. But unresolved and unexamined it can lead to bitterness, resentment and misunderstanding. Even the most skilful operator has no panacea for problem solving and conflict resolution, but there are many situations where his ability in this area can be a decisive factor for co-operation.

Education

There is a cluster of roles in our society where the incumbent straddles the divide between education and social work: the community worker is one of these. (In this context education may be said to be concerned with the sharing of knowledge and skill whilst social work is about helping the client to cope with his problems.) It is required that we see community projects as an aspect, though not the whole, of adult education. This is demonstrated in practice: the community worker needs the instinct and the methods of the educator. Success may depend on his insight into the possibilities for growth and development of the individuals he works with and his capacity for facilitating their progress.

Two educational opportunities and demands keep recurring. One is to make available, in a digestible form, the mass of information which local inhabitants must have if they are to be more active on their own behalf. This includes mundane items like knowing what grants and benefits are available in certain contingencies, who is the right official to talk to; but it widens into broader considerations like grasping how a local authority works and where are the structures of power. The second opening is in teaching social skills to a people who may previously have missed many benefits because they did not know how to approach an official, organize a campaign or complain in an effective and dignified way. Social deprivation and social ignorance often go together and reinforce each other. If this company were not socially needy it would not matter so much that they were socially inept; if they were more socially skilful they would have a better chance of satisfying their social needs. Part of the educational efforts of the community worker are directed to breaking this nexus. In many enterprises designed to improve the quality of social living it has now been seen that the best chance of success is an improvement in the organizational skills of those who are to be served. One good example is the attempt to make better provision for those adolescents who might be described as 'leisure-deprived'.[5]

'Education' in this country still carries the suggestion of formal arrangements with the set time and place and the teacher who knows and tells those who don't. Not that formal arrangements are to be ruled out entirely in the present context. I know of at least one 'shop floor' full-time community worker who decided that the next logical and relevant step was a course of lectures on social structure offered to the indigenous leaders who were emerging in his theatre of operations. The course was held in conjunction with the local WEA and was successful. Still, it remains true that most of his educational efforts will be informal, using the opportunities that arise in conversation, committees and crises.

> Men must be taught
> As if you taught them not.
> And things unknown proposed
> As things forgot.

Facilitating

This is patently related to the last skill but is given brief reference under a separate heading because in one respect at least it is identifiably different. In exercising educational skills the worker focuses his attention on a process of development: he is at that moment only indirectly concerned with the end product, the task achievement. But there is a use of facilitating skill which is more immediately concerned with results, with plans, with decisions. We can often watch the good facilitator at work with a group. He has made up his own mind on the issue and knows what he thinks would be the best course of action. But he is determined not to show his hand unless he is asked directly: even then he may avoid commitment since this could mean not merely that they will stop working at the problem for themselves but, even more serious, they are likely in the future always to think of the decision as his since they acted on his advice. Instead our good facilitator concentrates on encouraging the members to dig deep within themselves and discover their own resources. If he is compelled to intervene it is with remarks like 'I know you have views about this, Joe' and 'I wonder what Mary thinks of this, we have not heard from her yet' and 'How would that look to your people,

Geoff?' Under such promptings of a good facilitator it is a fact that many groups discover they know together more than they thought they knew, they have more power of decision and more courage to face the consequences of their own actions.

Co-operation

Running through these descriptions of the ability of the ideal community worker is the capacity to work with others at many levels. Negatively, this excludes the lone wolf and/or the leader who secretly enjoys the exercise of his own charisma and/or he who is so personally insecure that he needs the assurances which come from controlling other people and being in the centre of the picture. It is of course a personality type that in any case is not likely to survive for long in our kind of work. A more rewarding exercise then is to look at the positive constituents of the ability to co-operate.

We have already observed that some of those are described under other headings. Thus a worker is not likely to be good at co-operation unless he is good at communication and can encourage his colleagues to make their best contribution. But in addition there are important aspects of this competence on which so far there has been no concentration. Good co-operation means at least:

a Knowing when to be active and when to be passive, in other words making appropriate interventions. Too little support means the people will be crippled, too much means they will grow over-dependent and fail to develop their own considerable powers.

b Early identification of areas of integrated action between dissident groups or even those who are indifferent to each other.

c The capacity to see and suggest attempted solutions to problems which appear to be insoluble. Keen as we may be on self-determination, it is a contribution which is called for again and again. Leaders from one point of view are simply people who reach impasse later and less frequently than others. Of course, the worker will want the others, not just to take over his idea, but to explore and examine it for themselves: he may even succeed in letting them think that the idea came originally from them.

d The power and the skill to give a practical demonstration of how to work harmoniously with other people of differing ideologies and temperaments from one's own.

e   The attitude which in practical terms can unite tolerance and idealism, flexibility and stability. Effective workers in this context are idealists without illusions. What this means on the 'shop floor' is that the community worker is often beset by the opposing temptations of being so 'loyal to his vision' that he is seriously affected by the difficulties, the lack of response and so on: settling for despair, cynicism or a constant state of disgruntlement that is a threat to his health and a disturber of other folks' peace of mind: or, by contrast, the exigencies of his situation produce conformity to the reduced expectations of those around him, and complacency. A large element in his powers of co-operation depends on his own attitude in being able not to forget the primary goal whilst being able to accept and use what others are able to do, though they do not see the end so clearly, or if they do, don't like, as much as he does, what they see. Leaders are those who pity but go forward.

Training of the community worker

In describing the required skills of the community worker we have admittedly painted an ideal picture of a human being who nowhere exists. Perhaps if he is alive somewhere, one would not expect to find him in this type of employment. Similarly, when we come to indicate the type and method of training that is required, we are also driven to perfectionist and doctrinaire approaches in order to be comprehensive. But in this case, a further brake on our expectation is that these courses are likely to be of relatively short duration even for full-time community workers. At the most they will be two years. That is certainly not long enough, other considerations apart, to produce a superman.

Before we enter into detailed suggestions, notice is taken of one other issue. As we have seen, not everybody who has thought about the matter agrees that there ought to be courses of training, separate and distinct, for community workers. For example, there are those who consider that this training would find a more appropriate place as part of a general course in social work. We are not here entering into this controversy. What follows are suggestions for a full-time course for the training of community workers. This would have to be adapted to those situations where community work was seen as only part of the professional role for which the student was being prepared.

Aims of a training course

There are three intentions, separated for purposes of analysis and teaching, but in practice integrated in the course itself. In fact we are here putting asunder what in the nature of the case is joined together. The three elements are:

a   Academic   Being brought into touch with the relevant body of knowledge.

b   Personal development   The provision of experiences which will prompt the emotional maturation of the student.

c   Practical skill   Opportunities to be involved in community work projects, thereby enhancing one's ability to do the work. Before we look at the list in more detail it is worth observing that this pattern is shared with many other courses of training and preparation for helping roles. We can say, in fact, that in any society there are three kinds of labourers, each distinguished by the type of raw material with which they are principally engaged.

a   Those concerned primarily with ideas—the poets, philosophers and creative artists.

b   Those concerned primarily with things—the mechanics, factory operatives and others.

c   Those concerned primarily with people—the teachers and social workers for example.

We must hastily comment that these categories are not to be seen as absolute and watertight. The plumber's specialism, for instance, is with pipes but perhaps he will be a better plumber if he knows how to relate to the families whose homes he visits. Human relations in industry are recognized as an important aspect of production of goods.[6] So managers who might be placed in the first group began to show a marked resemblance to educationalists and social workers. Still, the brief typology is not without value since it helps us to distinguish three contrasted operatives in terms of their major orientation. The point we are making here is that for all of those in the third group, and not merely community workers, we could say that the threefold aim is knowledge, personal development and skill.

Content

There should then be constant interaction between these three phases: no single activity on the course should fit exactly into each 'box'. So, to take one example only out of a number of possibilities, the student who is engaged on an academic study of group dynamics will find that the theories he confronts are constantly tested by his own involvement with groups, as he will also find that his own emotional maturity is challenged by this participation.

However, we can for the moment pretend that they are separate in order to describe our best intentions under each heading.

Academic knowledge   The major concern is with the social sciences. It is simply an attempt to help the student to find a better answer to the question, 'Why do people behave as they do, whether as individuals or members of groups or communities?' But that shorthand version conceals a wide-ranging area of study. (Many students on entry to the course are found to have a primary need to be encouraged 'to think sociologically', that is, to interpret human behaviour partly in terms of solid pressures and not wholly in the light of individuality.) Hence it is a large subject and we lack the space for a detailed examination. The two Gulbenkian reports provide a meticulous and thoughtful examination of the subject. We can, however, indicate what ideally we would expect the student to gain from this part of his training. He should acquire, not a received body of knowledge which is not available, but a thoughtful tested insight into:

a   Human growth and development
b   Human relations
c   A sociological perspective
d   Modern understanding of 'community' and community processes
e   The administrative and political structures of our society
f   The recent history of community work

It is a formidable list and even the salient parts of it are only remotely possible by methods presently to be described.

Personal development   A quick overview of the skills required by the community worker, as described in the earlier part of this chapter, will disclose that again and again they make demands upon his character, personality, nervous resources and emotional maturity. It is the current fashion to minimize the part played by the social worker as a person in a laudable attempt to break away from the old image of the benevolent dictator relying upon his charismatic qualities. But an extreme stance on this matter can only be maintained at a distance remote from the theatre of operation. Real-life community workers require strength of character to sustain non-directive approaches. How far any such possibility can be organized on a course of training is a delicate matter. The most that can be hoped is that tutors may make possible certain experiences for the students in which they find themselves confronted by their own inadequacies and yet find that they are in a supportive and accepting atmosphere.

A tutor does this when he is available for personal counselling and is, at other times, ready to play the supervisory role when the student reflects upon the recording of his practical work. Even more frequently and effectively it happens among a group of students who meet regularly to help with each other's training. The tutor is obviously concerned to initiate and maintain a group process of learning and is not content to rely upon the communication system between himself and the student. What is true of all aspects of the training applies with special force here—progress comes by reflection upon personal experience. So much is this the case that, without anybody even trying to force the issues, a course of training for community work (as for other educational and social work roles) often has terrific consequences for the outlook, attitudes and personal philosophy of the student. We may not use here the word 'conversion' since it has religious connotations, but we may employ the sociologically more respectable word 'alternation'. This is a process by which we accept alternate interpretations of our major earlier experiences. As we remember the past we are all of us restructuring it in accordance with what we now think is important: it is the latter system which changes in the process of alternation.

More specifically, a student for whom the training has personal consequences may learn that the values he is seeking to impose on others have been provided for him by his own peculiar social experiences, or that his range of sensitivity is limited, or that he is far less unselfish than he supposed and is, in fact, unconsciously satisfying many of his own needs. Self-knowledge and self-acceptance have important implications for the day-to-day professional performance. They reduce the nervous strain and increase the margins of emotional strength: they facilitate non-judgmental approaches to the groups and individuals with whom one works.

So far we have looked at these possibilities from what might be described as a negative perspective. We have thought of the student being impelled to change his attitudes by finding himself in situations where he is brought face to face with his own needs and inadequacies. The process has been called in an unfortunate phrase, 'abrasive therapy'.

Possibilities of positive approaches to personal development should not be overlooked. This means the opportunity for the student to initiate or maintain an interest in a subject that has nothing directly to do with his professional life. There is a wide range of choices, depending upon individual preference, among the arts, sport and so on, but on the whole an interest calling for active participation is better than one offering passive enjoyment.

This demand will appear unrealistic to some, the provision of confectionery rather than bread and butter. On the contrary, we maintain that it is a practical matter evidenced by what happens to many community workers. The daily demands upon heart, mind and nerves can be heavy. There are the constant dangers of tiredness, over-involvement and intenseness. Happy are those who have—and we offer no apology for the term—a place of retreat: who realize that though everything matters nothing matters absolutely: who return refreshed and renewed to the daily grind from inhabiting a world which has nothing to do with their professional responsibilities. Known to the writer are many workers in this field a part of whose intriguing individuality is the particular way in which for a time they 'get away from it all'. One man grows chrysanthemums: another unwinds late at night by listening to Grieg's music: a third has become an expert on model trains.

Training programmes should not neglect this aspect; in aiming at professional competence they have to offer possibilities of learning to use leisure time in patterns of renewal.

Practice   At least half the time spent on the course should be experience of the work undertaken by community agencies. 'The purpose of fieldwork is to enable students to perceive in real life what they are studying theoretically, to apply this knowledge in order to acquire skill as community workers, and in doing so to develop more awareness of themselves and others, coupled with the appropriate attitudes and values.'[7] From the same page, we may usefully quote a more detailed list. The general aims [of fieldwork] are to enable students to have:

1   Experiences of working in an organization undertaking community work.
2   Knowledge and experience of a particular community, its problems and the organizations working in it.
3   Knowledge and experience of some of the social needs and forms of social provision with which community work is concerned.
4   Opportunities for the application of knowledge and principles to actual community situations.
5   Opportunities to develop the skills and techniques necessary for effective community work.
6   Opportunities to develop self-awareness and a disciplined use of the student's own personality as a helper in a variety of community work situations, flexibility of response to many different people and situations, as well as clarity about aims.

To which it is perhaps necessary to add only a few general considerations which govern this area of training.

a   A range of different fieldwork experiences should be provided varying according to:
  i   An assessment of the individual needs of students. Despite the pressures to support local enterprises by the use of training agencies' resources, the overriding consideration in choice of placements must be what appropriate learning possibilities exist for the student.
  ii   Placements should cover different levels of involvement for the student. In one instance, he may be only an observer, elsewhere he carries some responsibility for the work that is being attempted. In general, we may say that involvement will be increased in the later stages of his course.
  iii Choices of fieldwork situations should be made in the light of the student's need to develop two interrelated skills. One

is the ability to gather facts and make analytical judgments. The other is the power to make the relationships essential for his task.

iv   The foregoing carries the suggestion that all the decisions are in the hands of the tutor and may even have depicted him as an authoritarian figure. This is not intended. The student should be involved in the assessment of his own needs to the limit of feasibility and he should have a say in the decisions. One training course has discovered that if a group of students is to work together at the same agency, it is better for the composition of the team to be decided by the sociometric choices of the students themselves.

b   Efficient supervisory service is required to exploit the learning possibilities of fieldwork experiences. This means that the student has ample opportunities to reflect upon the deeper meanings of those experiences, aided by his recordings and by the pressure and intervention during the recall process of tutors and/or fellow students.

c   Careful choice should be made of the agencies to be used. This will be partly in the light of the circumstances of their operations but even more in the light of the qualities and potentialities of the officers working in them. They become colleagues of the tutors on the course and tutors in their own right. Long consultations are demanded to produce an effective partnership. But, for example, not all effective community workers are also effective tutors. The two gifts are quite separate and are not always lodged within the same personality. Some training courses offer training in tutorial and supervisory skills to the full-time community workers whose agencies they are using for fieldwork placements.

d   It is required to ponder deeply the procedures for assessment of each student's progress and the related matter of the evaluation of his course as a whole. It is not easy to construct valid standards of measurements and to exclude subjective elements, but the attempt must be made.

We have now concluded the section on the aims and contents of training. Looking back, it seems we may have minimized the difficulties and simplified the issues in a way that would certainly have been unacceptable had there been larger space for this section. Organizers of those courses face acute shortages in three areas. One is the lack of casework material from the British scene. Another is the dearth of suitable placements for students' fieldwork. The third is perhaps the most serious—the paucity of efficient supervisors and tutors. We have hinted above at the dilemmas which arise, for example, in the areas of assessment and evaluation. Readers who want to explore this issue at depth could begin by reading the relevant chapters in the two Gulbenkian reports.

Method of a training course

The structure of these courses and the educational approaches employed are nearly as important as the content. And of course the two cannot be separated. In talking about content we have found ourselves again and again talking about methods. That we have been compelled to do this suggests a deep connection between the two. Here, as elsewhere, it is not true to say that the ends justify the means: more accurately, the means determine the end. How a course is conducted eloquently demonstrates community-development principles or no less eloquently it denies them.

In the positive possibility, there is first the recognition of the active part which is to be played by the student in his own progress. Effective training is not something which can be imposed from outside: it comes from within when the trainee realizes his own needs. Nobody ever trains anybody else in the skill of human relationships, therefore, the frequent title 'trainer' is a misnomer: the hope is that students will train themselves using the resources which are made available. This implies the constant use of non-directive approaches by the authorities in all feasible areas that the student may be impelled to define his own needs rather than be told by an 'expert' what they are.

This also implies a further rigorous scrutiny of the role of the tutor. He is there not to provide answers to dilemmas from his experience and expertise, but to facilitate in-service experiences for the student by which he will be impelled into self-knowledge and learning. An ancient Chinese proverb expresses the possibilities neatly:

What I hear, I forget.
What I see, I remember.
What I do, I know.

Quite simply, then, the methods of the course should be an answer
to the questions: How can we facilitate significant community
work experiences for this trainee? How can we, where necessary,
impel him into those experiences? How can we help him to gain
the most from those experiences by reflection upon them? The
history of this type of course suggests that the answers lie in three
directions.

a   *Tutors*   The staffing ratio should allow the course for each
student not merely to be tailor-made, but *haute couture*: that is,
beyond the common elements for all, to be a special creation
designed for him alone. This results in a special relationship for
each student with tutor, covering personal, academic and practical progress. In fact, we are arguing for the Oxbridge tutorial
system to be applied to the training of community workers.

b   *Fellow-students*   All occasions, both informal and formal,
whereby trainees can look to each other—sharing success and
failure, sharing the insight gained from reading, practice and
seminars—should be encouraged and supported by those responsible for the courses. That is why tutors need to have group
skill as well as academic learning and one-to-one counselling
ability.

c   *Community agencies in the field*   Where the agency is to be used
for placements, the necessity of prolonged co-operation is obvious:
the workers in the agencies become partners with students and
tutors in the training process. But there is a wider opportunity
present even when the agency is not used for placement. The contact represents an educational experience for tutors and workers:
there should be a feed-back from community projects to training
establishments unless they are quickly and disastrously to be out
of touch: and the tutor can bring to local situations interpretations from a panoramic view which may be hidden from the
'shop-floor' operative.

The training position

There are today over one hundred centres where training is offered for professional community work, if the phrase is interpreted in its most general meaning. One way of classifying the provisions is to identify three categories:

a   Universities or polytechnics which are members of the Joint University Council.
b   Training institutions which offer courses associated with the Central Council for Education and Training in Social Work.
c   Other courses of training, for example in Youth and Community Work.

It is an impressive total and the spectacular growth in the number of courses offering this facility over the past five years reflects the mounting interest in the subject. But the bare recital of the quantity of courses conceals the dilemmas and confusion which beset this kind of training. It can cogently be argued that variety may be good. Not only does it correspond to the varying opportunities in the community today but it enables the applicant 'to shop around' until he finds the type of training which corresponds to his aspirations.

The force of this argument is reduced, however, when the variations are discovered to express, not rich variety, but lack of consultation, of integrated policies and a coherent philosophy. They could not even be said to share a common objective since some appear to work to train community work *per se* or to inform students of sociology and social administration, educationalists and casework of trainees of community-work theory and practice. It is hard to throw off the suspicion that in a few cases the organizers of these courses have climbed on a band wagon whose slogans they but imperfectly understand.

The basic confusion at the present time is a failure to agree on whether training for community work is a specialism in its own right or whether it is an aspect of a general training in social work. In practice a large majority of courses is located in the second possibility. It can be within this context a small part of the course, a larger 'optional extra', or the attempt at the training for a specialist skill in community work. There is of course a strong argument for all education and social workers being made aware of community work principles in preparation for their careers. But something else is intended, namely that these optional offers of specialisms within a more general course will be adequate to train the full-time community worker, whether he is concerned with local development possibilities or inter-agency work. When we look at the curricula of the various courses we find many variables in the amount of time devoted to seminars on community work or in the type, duration, function and structure of fieldwork placements. These all reach back to indecisiveness about the role of full-time community work in relation to other educational and social-work roles. It is required that we discern similarities and differences existing at the same time between two realities. Full-time community work calls for a recognition of its separateness and hence for the safeguard of a relative autonomy whilst at the same time provision should be made for formalizing its links with other educational and social-work provision. The Gulbenkian suggestion may prove to be the most feasible as well as the most attractive:[8] that is, an independent council to recognize and evaluate community work courses which should one day become part of a general co-ordination of social-work provision by having relative autonomy in the Central Council for Education and Training in Social Work.

Meanwhile, there is hope and promise in the mounting experience of the 'trainers' and in the growing body of casework material both on the operations of community-work projects and training for them. What is needed now is attempts to gather and co-ordinate this material—far more opportunities for consultation among those concerned and attempts to work out agreed philosophies and approaches. Indirectly this could be going a long way to meet that other crying need for in-service training of people involved at all the many different levels of community work.

At present there is a rich diversity in training as a practice: the next step is to compare notes and discover if possible the strength and purpose that lies in unity. The first Gulbenkian report hoped that the next few years would be a concentration on a 'few centres of excellence' in training so that more could be learned in this way. Events overtook this hope. Nothing could stem the flood of new courses. We cannot do otherwise than try to navigate in the new circumstances.

5 Why the present interest in community work?

As we have said, there is nothing new about community work: it has a long history and has many times in the past been attempted by teachers, social workers, clergy and missionaries among others. The latter part of the nineteenth century in this country contained numerous examples of mutual-aid movements. Men and women taking part did not talk about group conflict and interaction: nor did they have the analytical tools by which today we seek to estimate success and failure. But in their own time, they were community workers and when we read their biographies, we find, perhaps to our surprise, that their problems and opportunities were curiously like our own.

Interest in community work

Yet there is a difference. 'Community' is a word more widely and frequently used today: it attracts a fresh enthusiasm and offers a new dimension of interpretation. As we observed in the preface, it has become a fashion to talk about it: with some, we may suspect, it is even a fad. There is a preoccupation with the concept both as the subject of intellectual enquiry and as a practical means of government. We are likely to run into the word whichever way we turn. In 1972 two English by-elections were won—uncharacteristically—by the Liberal candidates. The political commentators agreed that both had succeeded by the use of 'community politics', whatever that means. There are few days when the news bulletins escape the use of the word. As we have seen, a new profession is growing up around the exercise and many older, more established professions are being profoundly affected by the ethos of the approach. The first study group of the Gulbenkian committee thought that the idea had become so fashionable that there was a real danger of ill-prepared, ill-considered and inadequate training courses being offered as qualifications.

The interest is by no means confined to Britain. Indeed, under the pressure of dire necessity, it is at least talked about even more in many developing countries. (We shall presently examine more precisely the similarities and differences of the notion in the two contrasted situations.) In the Caribbean and African countries, in the Philippines, Greece and Sardinia, the only hope for an improvement in the quality of life is seen to lie in self-help activities. India's successive five-year plans have a major dependence upon a process of community development to bring change to backward and traditional villages. Help from outside, from the richer countries of the earth, certainly in all the forms that have been common so far, can, tragically and ironically, make matters worse. Educational programmes produce thousands of men not willing to work on the land (which is what the economy requires) and searching vainly for jobs which match their qualifications. Technological innovations swell the ranks of the unemployed. These countries can be served only by labour-effective programmes. Massive aid programmes conceal the fact that it is goods which are transferred and goods which suit the economy of the donor rather than the recipient: and that much 'aid' is in fact 'loans'. The path of progress lies in the encouragement to develop their own resources. This is the declared policy of international agencies like the United Nations, the International Labour Office and the Commonwealth Secretariat. And this is why an acknowledged authority on the subject can write in this vein. Gunnar Myrdal is emphatic for a review of present practice in the light of these principles: 'Last but not least, it is needed to give the support that true knowledge can give to the liberal forces in underdeveloped countries which, against heavy odds, are struggling for domestic reforms.'[1]

An international sounding, then, is one way to read the present interest in community work. But, by contrast, another is to consider the heterogeneity of the people concerned about this issue with whom one is brought into close contact. They are a motley crew. There is clearly not one single personality type attracted by these notions: they represent contrasted approaches to life. One suspects that there are those among them who are primarily motivated by nostalgia: they want to restore something which they feel has been lost. More, however, are driven by radicalism: they want to reach out to something which they feel men have never had. Discontent is the one common factor: they are brought together by a conviction that life at present is not what it should or could be and they direct their efforts to redressing a balance. We are concerned now to examine the reasons for the present concern, since we believe the community workers should have a grasp of the historical and philosophical reasons for the strength of the present efforts. Part of the evidence for that concern is among the community workers and the many aspects of their diversity.

We shall confine our attention to Britain, though there is a broad similarity in this matter between all the developed countries in the democratic tradition. With a few national variations they face the task of securing maximum efficiency to confront modern problems whilst refusing to surrender to the temptation to impose totalitarian controls on the population. Communist countries, for example, display on the whole an impressive solidarity and secure a high level of co-operative effort from the citizens. But there are nations who consider the price too high and that the loss of the fruitfulness of dissent is not adequately compensated. On a visit to an East Berlin youth centre, the warden told me, 'Our aim in the German Democratic Republic is to have all the voices in the youngster's life saying the same thing to him—home, State, school and later industry.' The three points on the neckerchief of the Young Pioneers represent the first three educative influences. One may contrast that with the fragmentation of the socializing forces, for adults as well as for children, in the democracies. Agencies with important socializing functions have disparate goals, different levels of operation and are relatively independent of each other. Yet even the democracies are required by the conditions of survival to have some unity of purpose. But they want to reach it by discussion that does not exclude dissent, by attempts at consensus rather than controls imposed from above. The process of community development is an encouragement of and a contribution to this immensely difficult task—made more difficult because the democracies are passing through a period of rapid social change.

Reaction to social change is the factor which unites the efforts in the developing and developed countries. In the first instance, the introduction of technology may act clean contrary to the traditional patterns of life and may tear the social fabric. A sudden leap from the hoe to the tractor can have serious social and human consequences. I well remember seeing some families watching television programmes in Hong Kong. They were occupying some of the first flats put up for the flood of migrants from Communist China. The early provision was 100 square feet as the total living space for a whole family. One could not help speculating on the effects of this view of the wider world from their narrow confines. That is a parable of what has happened in many parts of the world where western technical man has come to primitive societies bearing gifts that contain immense promise and immense threat.[2] The promise is that the underprivileged may have at least the basic necessities of life—enough food, clean water supply, proper sanitation, medical services, education and job prospects. But the poor people of the world are learning to be suspicious of those who come bearing gifts. One reason only is the danger that in accepting the gifts they will lose their 'souls', that is forfeit the cultural traditions and beliefs and patterns of social interaction which provide corporate and individual identity, emotional security and other psychological benefits not always apparent in western culture. For the developing countries, the community-development process, under the impact of social change, is the organized attempt not to allow technological innovation to ignore social and cultural consequences: this is attempted through programmes of community education so that changes may come from 'below' and not be imposed from 'above'. But in the poorer countries the exigencies of the situation demand that a primary motive be the supply of the basic necessities. It is not quite like that in the developed countries. True, the pressures there also arise from the impact of social change, as later we shall see in more detail. But though there are large pockets of serious economic deprivation in richer countries and though these are admittedly the proper concern of community work—yet here the social, psychological and mental health needs of the people fill a larger part of the picture. It is not that either emphasis is entirely absent from either situation, but the variation in stress is con- siderable. In the western democracies for the most enthusiastic— some would say naïve—advocates, community development is a method of breaking through the apathy, frustration and impersonal quality of these cultures, rescuing many modern people from debilitating loneliness and isolation and giving them a sense of belonging and a worthwhile purpose. Rich countries can afford to indulge a larger concentration on the spiritual quality of individual life. Lawrence Stenhouse has described one part of the differential we have identified. 'Typically, mass culture does not provide a basis for rich relationships and does not fortify private thinking. The words, symbols and images given to us by the mass communication are not good tools of discourse and of thought, because they overdetermine our reactions. They prejudice us rather than liberate us.'[3] That is undoubtedly true: and in Britain it is a proper concern for those who wish to encourage community development: but in the world at the present time, it is a luxury to be able to devote attention and resources to it. Among the poorer members of the human family, who constitute the majority, community work must be orientated to the provision of the basic necessities of life—food, water, sanitation, shelter, work, health—whilst also being concerned to prevent the impact of western technology from being socially and culturally destructive.

Before passing on, one last feature of the relationship is worth noting. Community-development intentions and programmes in the developing part of the world have proved to be the inspiration and prototype of similar schemes among the richer relations. What was useful on the wrong side of the tracks was surprisingly seen to have relevance for suburbia.

In developing countries the ideal intentions of community work seem to take into account three realities.[4] One is that the vast energies of under-employed population can be deployed for schemes of material benefit: where every other resource is scarce, manpower is plentiful and may be harnessed to the common good. The second is that the approach encourages active participation and thus aids in the fight against social and economic dependence and provides experience of the democratic process. Lastly, it helps to cushion societies which have been static for centuries against the more disastrous consequences of sudden social change and provides the institutions on which social change depends, like women's clubs and youth centres and village halls.

The single point which is being made here is that though by no means all hopes have been fulfilled, yet these approaches have met with a measure of success among the poorer nations: so much so that the question was asked whether there was not an object lesson here for the complex industrial nations. Perhaps this was a means for them to generate enthusiasm, dispel apathy and foster corporate feeling. Paradoxically, it came to be supposed that the treatment which had helped Dives might be suitable for Lazarus.

Events in the ecclesiastical sphere are part illustration and part patterns of parallel progression. In short, the ecumenical movement in Britain and elsewhere received powerful impetus from schemes of union in the Third World. The Anglicans and the Methodists came together in the Church of South India long before there were any serious and formalized conversations about the union of the two churches in this country. From the perspective of the Christian ideology, fragmentation and disunity made even less sense in the Third World where the churches were confronted with the powerful counter-attractions of strong faiths like the Muslim and Hindu. Moreover, denominationalism had grown in western societies: it is a product of historical forces and is a curious blend of social, economic, psychological and doctrinal differences. In exporting denominationalism, the missionaries were imposing an indigenous pattern on an alien environment. With the benefit of hindsight, we can now observe that the progression was logical and predictable. Ecumenical movements among 'the churches overseas' gave powerful impetus to similar movements among 'the churches at home'. And this was consistent with one feature of the relationship between community development in the two contrasted situations.

Asking the question 'why?'

In returning to the main theme of this chapter, we can observe that our topic is an example of a major specialism of sociologists. They in fact are always asking the question 'why?' Their concern is to look at social phenomena and ask what purpose is being served by these events and this behaviour. And in performing this office they are frequently driven to reject the popular answers as not being a complete account of the affair: in technical language, they often have to disregard the manifest functions of social behaviour and look for the latent functions. The 'folk image' about Bonfire Night is that we are remembering the deeds of one Guy Fawkes. But the sociologist may not be satisfied with the adequacy of this explanation of the survival of a curious, costly and dangerous celebration. He may wonder whether part of a deeper explanation may not lie in the fact that secret pyromaniac tendencies are fairly widespread among the population and it is socially useful and tension-relieving to set aside one day in the year when such behaviour is acceptable. Why is the celebration of a religious festival like Christmas kept up among a people who, by and large, have ceased to practise the Christian religion? Perhaps part of the answer is that there are vestigial remnants of faith even among those who have clearly drifted from the religion of their fathers. But cursory investigation shows that Christmas is useful for individuals and society. It provides cheer at the darkest season; offers a break in the daily routine; fosters a sense of community where many feel imprisoned in their private world; facilitates social contact; expresses, strengthens and sometimes re-establishes family ties.

Sociologists are charged by the ethos of their vocation to eschew supernatural, chance and irrational explanations of social events and to ask, 'what purpose is served in this society by these things?'[5]

All that concerns us here is that the present widespread interest in community work requires an explanation that is not merely mystical or ideological but contains elements of a sociological critique. We shall expect to find both manifest and latent functions served in the present enthusiasm. Another reasonable explanation is that the present emphasis will spring from a multiplicity of causes. A break-through on the human front is usually found to occur at the meeting place of many forces.

A short answer

An answer to our question in one sentence would be: An increasing number of people are motivated to think and act in the area of community work because they consider this to be a relevant response to the fact that in modern Britain there are conditions leading for many to an impoverishment in the quality of living— economically, socially, psychologically and spiritually.

This has the merit of brevity and is broad enough to include all who are in the field, both philosophers and workers. But it still fails to call attention to general features of the endeavour.

Ross provides a five-point rationale of community work:[6]

i   Every advance of industry has so far been accompanied by a corresponding impoverishment in social living.
ii The processes of urbanization have almost destroyed man's feeling of belonging 'to a community'.
iii It is hard to maintain social unity under modern conditions.

iv The development of large sub-groups in modern societies leads to tension.

v New ways of living call for new forms of democratic institutions.

Two assumptions lie behind this list. First, they represent needs for which community work attempts provision. The fact is that modern societies do not give to many of their citizens the psychological support they need, or call significantly for the help of the citizens. Industrialized societies are in marked contrast to their predecessors since they do far less to define the total role and status of the individual as a human being and hence he is thrown upon his own psychological resources. The point has often been made by writers on the subject but nowhere better than by Stein.[7]

> Primitive community life can be viewed as a set of arrangements for protecting the integrity of the individual life cycle. Guarantees of a share of the necessities of life are an integral part of the meaning of tribal membership. More importantly, the tribe guarantees a share of emotional necessities by providing ritual celebrations of the phases of life. The shared drama of human life—the potentialities inherent in each phase of the life cycle, masculinity and femininity, the passions, ambivalence, man's yearning for omnipotence, his dependence on others and his quest for identity—are the points of primitive community life.

The second supportive assumption behind Ross's list is the reality of rapid social change. Families have to cope with new conditions like living in a flat, or on a housing estate or in a twilight area. But it is not only a question of coping with the changes: a conviction is growing that more people should participate in the decisions which determine the direction of social change.

We can guess the total effects by considering one aspect only of the many-sided topic of social change: and that is mobility. This comes in three types, all of them determinative for the lives of families:

a *Geographical* We are less likely today to live all our days in the same house, neighbourhood or even region. Internal migration results in the movement of large sections of the population to towns and cities. External migration has brought over one million commonwealth citizens to live in Britain during the past twenty years.

b *Social* We are less likely to stay in the socio-economic stratum where we began life. The wider spread of educational opportunity leads to a higher rate of social mobility if the matter is judged on the grounds of occupation.

c *Vocational* We are less likely to stay in the same job all our lives. Economic developments have already led to a massive switch of employment: the number of re-training schemes keeps growing: the trend is likely to become more marked in the next few decades.

It should be stressed that mobility is only one of several aspects of social change which have serious implications for the private citizen. Many of the old stabilities are undermined. Men who thought they were 'settled for life' suddenly find themselves made 'redundant'. On the practical level we need to be protected from and learn how to adjust to the impact of social change. More idealistically, we should have opportunities of controlling, guiding, even initiating and deciding about innovations. Basically, community work mechanisms are designed for these ends.

Great Britain

Economic

Of course the material standards of living in Britain have, for the overwhelming majority, improved out of all recognition in the post-war period. But there is a darker side to this rosy picture. A not insignificant minority is trapped in pockets of painful deprivation. The conclusion of a recent survey[8] suggested that there are at least 100,000 homeless people in Britain. We are slowly learning the bitter lesson that in an affluent society the poor become poorer. This is partly, though not wholly, due to the fact that poverty to a large degree is relative. A man without a radio today would be counted poor indeed. But that would not have been so forty years ago. There is, however, a more sombre reality. An affluent society forces up the price of goods until the poor often cannot afford the basic necessities. There are some old-age pensioners for example who, in a hard winter, will not be able to buy enough fuel to keep warm enough to survive.

Community work cannot pretend directly to increase the size of the Gross National Product. But there are two ways in which it can make a salient contribution to the situation we have been describing. One is to evoke community awareness and response as part of a comprehensive plan for improvement in the conditions of life for the deprived. The belief still persists, and in the opinion of many observers is still the dominant view of public opinion, that the poor should overcome poverty themselves. But this essentially conservative interpretation fails to take account of the truth that under modern conditions this is precisely what the poor cannot do. Nor is the balance redressed by an increase in the Gross National Product or by an insistence on equal rights. But a substantial hope lies in a wide awareness of the plight of the under-privileged and the acceptance of responsibility for them which issues in the appropriate forms of community action. At this point value-loaded language cannot be avoided. Community work is the attempt to give practical expression for an affirmative answer to the ancient question 'Am I my brother's keeper?'

The twin responsibility lies in the area of communication. Again and again it is discovered that the economically deprived in Britain do not know their rights or the benefits which have been made available for them by the State. And where they are dimly aware of these benefits, they do not know how to obtain them. It is hard to throw off the suspicion that in many cases public authorities do not strive too strenuously to inform them about either the provision or the means to obtain them. By this omission there is a saving of public money. First-hand accounts of their activities by 'grass roots' community workers show them spending a lot of their time at this task. They acquire for themselves the knowledge of welfare and social services' provision which is often complex, complicated and couched in language not easily understood. Then they pass on this information to the beneficiaries through neighbourhood newspapers or by word of mouth in personal encounters. But their duty does not end with the dissemination of the facts about information. We see them engaged, in various ways, in enabling the people to secure these benefits. This happens by working with individuals or groups, sometimes accompanying them to the encounter with the official concerned or teaching them how to do it for themselves or helping to fill in the form or write the necessary letter.

Social

Here we have to focus attention on a recurring theme of these reflections. Modern conditions—particularly in the urban locale—do not encourage community feeling: they do not foster in the individual the conviction that he belongs to his fellows.

The typical urban style supports the formal and functional interactions between people at the expense of the informal and expressive. Homans has explored the subject[9] in a manner that has been illuminating for subsequent consideration. When people are together for any length of time, there are at least two aspects of the association. One is what Homans calls the 'external system', that is the task which they have to perform together. The other is the 'internal system', the sentiments which they have about each other, the expressive content of their association. Modern conditions of urbanized living expand the first element and contract the second. They encourage privatism. There are more personal encounters where the essential content is functional, task-related rather than person-orientated and expressive. I know villages in Yorkshire where a visit to the local shop is a community experience. One acquires the local news and gossip. One is known as a person rather than a customer. Most of the conversation that takes place has nothing to do with the purchase and the shopkeeper may have to make a self-conscious effort to return to the business. 'See, what was it you came in for?' or, 'Well, I suppose I must get on with your list.' We may contrast that with a similar operation typical of the urban style. If a man buys a newspaper at a busy London railway terminal, the exchange is of a largely contractual nature. The assistant may have no time for a friendly reassuring smile or even to offer the brief courtesy of thanks for the purchase and the money. In a supermarket the atmosphere is brisk, efficient and impersonal.

One of the value assumptions behind community work is that a society sustained by a sense of unity and solidarity, whatever the tangible benefits, is to be preferred to one which is merely a collection of individuals. 'A society is healthier for a wide diffusion among its members of the experience of friendship in some depth, and where this is made difficult for particular people society is to that extent the loser through the emotional impoverishment of its members.'[10]

Psychological

If our description of the frequent style of life in modern Britain is accurate, then there are also aspects of it which represent an emotional loss for the individual. Loneliness, isolation, inadequacy and lack of identity may be the results for some. There is plenty of evidence to suggest that this is so and not only in the mounting incidence of mental illness of the population. Social workers report on the devastating loneliness suffered by many of their clients. A coffee bar set up in a London street to make contact with alienated teenagers was at first embarrassed by the number of isolated adults who wanted to use the service. Modern societies are less likely than their traditional predecessors to provide individuals with a meaning for their personal lives, a purpose to share and the realities which are attached—significance and identity.

Running through the writings about community development there is, paradoxically, a concern for the emotional experience of the individual. According to Biddle it 'should help the participants to achieve a more meaningful existence, to become more responsive to human needs, and to become more competent to live harmoniously with neighbours'.[11] The Gulbenkian report (p. 80) agrees with this humane intention and in two sentences manages to indicate the need and the hope of satisfaction.

> The essence of community work is an effort to relate factors making for change in society to the inherent general needs of persons including their need for stable and congenial relationships with other persons. In pursuit of this general goal it may often be necessary to press for such practical aids to well-being as better housing, better working conditions, and higher standards of living.

Moral and spiritual

Widely divergent views are expressed about the moral state of the nation. There would be a fair consensus for the view that the old moral systems have to be re-examined since they no longer have power over the masses. 'God and country' are not the rallying cries that once they were. We do not appear at the moment to be offered any exciting moral vision or task. Yet it may be doubted whether a nation can survive in a moral vacuum.

This is a place to tread delicately. But the question is raised, not always explicitly, whether community development has a contribution to make in the area. There are those who judge emphatically that it has. In brief, they would say that it is worth struggling towards the vision of a society that is compassionate, just and participant. With a passion that is reminiscent of the eighth-century prophets they denounce a society which often does not seem to care what happens to the old, the sick, the handicapped, the not-so-clever, the disorganized who cannot cope with their hard circumstances. Equally, they regard community development as the only sincere expression of political democracy in Britain today.[12]

> In a country such as ours, subject to the changes consequent upon a rapidly developing technology, society needs to engage in an intensive and perpetual transformation of itself, unless it is to respond to tomorrow's world with yesterday's activities and modes of organization. Our commitment is to a society in which every member can be publicly active: for only in this way can society become positively responsive to them, and, in the constant renewal of itself, reflect their values.

Urbanization, bureaucratization and industrialization

In describing the aspects of modern living which can lead to impoverishment, problems and dilemmas, we have found three 'regulation villains' who keep appearing in successive scenes on the stage. They are urbanization, bureaucratization and industrialization. Clearly they have important parts to play and they figure prominently in the drama of developed countries. Each of them is predictable in the light of technological advances. But before we consider how they are thought to contribute to the present needs, there is one important facet of their contribution. They are villains, but they are not unmitigated scoundrels. Each has a heart.

Each brings great gifts to men as well as threats. Each contains functional elements of response to a new situation.

Urbanization is a process by which human beings move from sparsely populated rural areas into densely populated conurbations. Since it is a world-wide phenomenon, it obviously contains attractions. To take any one example, the thousands who have forsaken the hill villages of Jamaica to huddle into Western Kingston with its overcrowding, poor housing conditions and massive unemployment, have been drawn by something. Here the bright lights, the amenities and commercial entertainment are a large part of the answer. Elsewhere, the opportunity to live one's life free from the restrictive controls of public opinion in a small community would be more prominent. In certain respects individuation is more feasible in the urban setting.

Again, in common parlance 'bureaucracy' is a dirty word but it is not difficult to show that on the modern scene it is not only inevitable but contains elements of social justice. Just because it is impersonal, it is non-discriminatory: it requires that officials distribute benefits in accordance with agreed rules and not as favours based on their whims. We are still indebted to Max Weber for his penetrating analysis of bureaucratization in modern societies.[13] 'Bureaucracy has a rational character: rules, means, ends, and matter-of-factness dominate its bearing.' It involves the objective discharge of business according to calculable rules and without regard for persons (p. 216).

> The more complicated and specialized modern culture
> becomes, the more its external supporting apparatus demands
> the personally detached and strictly 'objective' *expert*, in
> lieu of the master of older social structures, who was moved
> by personal sympathy and favour, by grace and gratitude.

Industrialization too has its brighter side since it has made a wide range of goods available to the masses and has therefore in some ways contributed to an improvement in the material standards of living. It has also contributed to social mobility and has given prominence to achieved status where a man's standing among his fellows depends more upon his talents and what he has made of them, and correspondingly less upon the given circumstances which are his by birth and inheritance.

These are some of the things that can be said in defence of

'the terrible triplets': but the bill of indictment is long and severe.

Urbanization

Frankenberg offers a balanced view on this subject whilst still expressing a strong personal preference.[14]

> I am not arguing that village life is 'better' than that of the town. . . . Nor however, do I personally believe that the life of English towns or cities is perfect and cannot be improved. . . . In my view the gains of urban life, actual and potential, are infinitely greater than the losses. I would rather have enough cubic feet of housing space and an efficient milkman than three acres of land and a cow.

Yet earlier (p. 275) he has neatly summarized what could be, in the minds of many people, features of the baleful effects of the situation for the urban dweller. 'In terms of role-theory he may be said to be role-confused: in terms of Durkeim's division of labour–anomic: in terms of Marxian proletarianization–alienated.'

The conviction that life somehow deteriorates in the town and city goes back a long way in history. It is a theme of the Old Testament. There were always those who thought that things had never been the same since the children of Israel entered the Promised Land: it was inevitably associated with the struggle for material gain and commercialism. Picturesquely, it is described as 'a-whoring after strange gods'. These prophets are always longing for the nomadic days when life was poorer, more primitive, beset by danger and uncertainty but somehow better. A famous struggle between two brothers is, one suspects, not only a family tale, but symbolizes the confrontation between these two forces in Jewish philosophy. Esau is a country lad, slow, ruled by bodily appetites, but loyal and trusting. Jacob by contrast is the 'city-slicker', clever, shrewd, ambitious and with not much depth, at least in his early days.

Curiously, there are modern counterparts of these traditionalists among an ancient people. In modern Israel there are active protesting sects who deplore the present developments including urbanization. In the USA one is constantly meeting people who pine for the good old days and who contrast the homely virtues of the countryside with the destructive and unimaginable vices of the great cities. Even the progressive radicals are often found to be arguing for a renewal of the old pre-urbanization values.[15]

Whatever its ultimate justification there are several parts to this ancient and persisting judgment, that life somehow is better in the country and that urbanization represents a measure of de-humanization. One has to do with individual experience. In the country the tempo of life is reduced: there is more time to stand and stare: there is more opportunity to reflect upon the deeper meanings of our existence: there is an accommodation to the rhythm of nature of which we are part. Equally, it is felt that rural dwellers have better chances to develop truly human relationships. Again, there is more time but no less stress is laid on the fact that the lives of people living in a village touch at many points and their links are far less likely to be functional and contractual than is the case in cities. Mass society can have many depersonalizing effects. Whilst it is true that the anonymity of city life permits the expression of individual talent, it leaves the individual vulnerable to isolation. Cowper was sure that 'God made the country, man made the town'. Probably Oscar Wilde characteristically had tongue in cheek when he remarked, 'Anybody can be good in the country', but Dryden sings with evident sincerity:[16]

> How blessed is he who lives a country life,
> Unvex'd with anxious cares, and void of strife!
> Who studying peace, and shunning civil rage,
> Enjoyed his youth and now enjoys his age:
> All who deserve his love, he makes his own:
> And, to be loved himself needs only to be known.

It must not be supposed that we are subscribing to these idyllic interpretations of the rural scene. We have already observed that there is, by those who have researched the subject, a modification of urban disadvantages. Conversely, the village can exhibit dep-rivation, neglect, privilege and bad feelings. There is a twofold point to be made. The relative merits of town and village are seen by many people in these or similar terms and social reality is what people see to be such. Equally, from professional social observers there would be support for the view that among undoubted gains, the emphatic trend towards urbanization in this century represents at least temporary loss. Moreover what has been lost is something that makes us distinctively human.

Bureaucratization

There are many factors about modern countries which make bureaucracy—in the Weberian, non-pejorative sense—inevitable and functional. Technology, the increase in the population and the enhancement in the material standards of living—all these conspire to make necessary central planning and central planners. Moreover, complex systems grow out of specialization and the division of labour: bureaucratic organization is essential for their administrative efficiency. So technical and interlocked are many of the issues which affect all our lives today that we are required to vest authority in the hands of those who have become experts in these matters. Administrative bureaucrats are required because there are so many of us and we are affected by so many organizations that an approximation to justice requires that we make rules and appoint officials to keep them. With this in mind it is worth reminding ourselves of the features which Weber had in mind when he offered his 'ideal type' or extended definitions of bureaucracy:[17]

a Fixed areas of official jurisdiction governed by laws and regulations.
b Offices organized on the basis of a clear hierarchy of authority.
c Administration based on written documents and conducted according to procedures for which special training is required.
d Personally free officials appointed on the basis of technical qualifications.
e Appropriation of neither office nor the means of administration by the official who is employed full-time and subject to strict discipline.
f A career for the official in which promotion is governed by seniority or merit, and a fixed salary paid according to rank.

Bureaucracy it will be seen is a device specifically constructed to exclude bribery and corruption of officials, favouritism and whimsical, unprofessional judgments. Why then has it acquired a bad name in the modern period? The answer is that despite its

G

indispensable excellencies, bureaucracy has acquired features which can seriously affect the quality of life for individuals and society.

In truth its faults are serious and call for considerable safeguards in a democracy. Bureaucracy can be wasteful of resources, both human and material: it can produce inflexibility and a loyalty that is restricted to a profession and its own structure: it is often impervious to the messages which come from outside.

But from our perspective the worst effect of bureaucracy is where its impersonal nature leads to depersonalization and dehumanization. Impersonality for the benefit of just dealing can be a fateful exchange at too high a price. Many people who are brought into touch with officials feel they 'are treated like dirt', whereas the officials themselves would think they are genuinely only 'following the rules', and doing their duty.

At another level, bureaucracies characteristically issue orders from above which filter to those below. It is often felt that in many cases the authorities have no true knowledge of the circumstances and needs of those who receive the judgments because they are too busy to learn or do not want to learn or there are no workable mechanisms of communications to let them know what is happening 'down below'. In autumn 1972 the Prime Minister was delayed by a traffic jam on a journey from the House of Commons to 10 Downing Street. He was compelled, by the exigencies of his appointments, to walk between the two buildings —a distance of about a quarter of a mile. As a result, he pressed the city authorities to speed their plans for coping with the traffic problems of London. Many commentators at the time enquired whether it required this personal experience to make him realize the daily frustration of many Londoners. During the same period a 'freeze' made illegal an increase in the price of most goods in the shops. Customers who encountered increases were invited to complain to the manager or ring up a government department. Whoever framed this optimistic advice cannot have realized that many people lack the confidence to complain to a manager and that many more not only do not have a telephone but are not used to using one. Bureaucracy may guard us against unfair discrimination and favouritism but it finds difficult the task of personalizing the social and educational services. There is a well-known story of some visiting Europeans in the 1950s watching a display by a light artillery crew. They were impressed by the precision and speed of the performance but intrigued by the sight of one man who simply stood to attention throughout. When they asked why he was there nobody knew the answer. It took a lot of searching through old army manuals to find out. He was the one who held the horses. Presumably nobody had ever asked the crew about the matter.

There are several features of a situation where it is felt that those who make the rules do not understand what is happening to those who have to keep the rules. One is the realization that there are occasions when the only means we have of finding out what people's true needs are is to ask them. The growth of consumer organizations and recent legislation on fair trading express this realization. Another is the tendency for central government to make laws which apply to regions without taking sufficient account of local conditions. The re-structuring of local government is partly designed to strengthen local administrative and political structures. The community councils hope to secure popular participation in public issues. The last felt weakness of present bureaucracy is its tendency towards a narrowing and fragmenting specialism. It produces experts who can propound schemes which efficiently provide for one need but to the neglect, or even the intensification, of other needs. Some of them in the past have built housing estates with little or no provision for the social needs of the dwellers, or they have built blocks of high-rise flats with no thoughts for the psychological health of families who live in them. A minimum requirement of the future is that these experts should seek to take account of the whole man and should, from the early stages, work in co-operation with experts in other relevant fields.

Industrialization

We cannot put the Industrial Revolution of Britain in a bracket of dates: it is a continuing process. Undoubtedly it has produced benefits for the masses as well as for the capitalists. The purchasing power of wages has increased out of all recognition: mass production has made available a wide choice of goods: there have come more opportunities for social mobility. But that there is a darker side is evident by the habit of some writers to indict the Industrial Revolution as the cause of our present malaise. Many of the con-

ditions of industrial labour are seen to contribute to depersonalization and the decaying of human relations on several grounds. They
set some men with immense power over others and they are considered to give some men the power of exploiting others. The
work itself is considered to be less meaningful, often repetitive,
calling for little inititaive and frequently offering little sense of
fulfilment. At their worst modern labour conditions are seen to
contribute to dehumanization and alienation. They are in the opposite position from the artist, happy to be hungry in his garret,
because it is the work itself which gives him satisfaction. In the
film *Modern Times*, Charlie Chaplin gave us a picture of the
assembly-belt worker which we are not likely to forget. Here was a
human being reduced, in the work situation at least, to little more
than a cog in a machine.

Two theoreticians, Marx and Durkheim, have exerted a major
influence on twentieth-century thought about the significance of
work in an industrial society, though their views have not gone
totally unchallenged or modified: many indeed would think that
the development of industrial societies beyond the life-span of the
first has belied some of his conclusions. Karl Marx[18] (1828–83)
thought that since in a capitalist society the worker is alienated
from his work in the sense that he neither gains satisfaction from
doing it nor receives the full product of his labours, he is also
alienated from his true nature as a man. His daily chores, by their
nature and setting, prevent him from exercising his creative
powers and releasing the full potentialities of his nature. There are
passages of Marx which, unexpectedly perhaps, are moving
expressions of the loftiest and most noble liberal sentiments.[19]

> A spider conducts operations that resemble those of a weaver,
> and a bee puts to shame many an architect in the constructions
> of his cells. But what distinguishes the worst architect
> from the best of bees is . . . that the architect raises his
> structure in imagination before he erects it in reality.

Separated from both the means and the fruit of production,
engaged not in a finished product but a simple mechanical operation, industrial man, according to Marx, cannot be himself.

Émile Durkheim (1858–1917) was centrally concerned with a
feature of industrial societies which was in marked contrast to the
style of pre-industrial days—the division of labour consequent

upon the specialization of function. In the old days, in societies characterized by little division of labour, solidarity rested upon shared interests and values among a people whose work was similar and undifferentiated, where people laboured together at group tasks and where skills were general and interchangeable. In an industrial society solidarity has a more functional and contractual basis depending upon the interdependence of the parts.[20]

Contemporary symbols of the ideas of Marx and Durkheim are exhibited often by people who do not know their origin. The signs are not less significant when they are as little as a human hand, like small clouds on the horizon that presage a change in the weather. The trade unions have always been concerned about 'conditions of work' as well as wages, but there are indications that this feature is being carried a stage further. Already in the USA there has been a labour dispute concerned, not with rates of pay, but with pressure to reduce the rate of rationalization processes and break up the monotony of working on the assembly line. Encouraged by rumours from Yugoslavia and elsewhere, there is talk today, not merely of 'the psychology of industry' and 'human relations in industry', but of a pattern of industrial democracy which gives the shop-floor worker more say in the policy-making decisions. Despite present pressures, it is being realized more and more that industrial troubles, perhaps unconsciously, are rooted in the psychological conditions of work as well as in the demands for more money.

Urbanization, bureaucratization, industrialization, these three, have affected profoundly the psychological and social experience of modern man. And in some respects, it is widely felt, for the worse. What then? They have happened and nothing can put the clock back. In general, then, the aim of community work may be said to be to look for the best of both worlds, to accept the gains of these three powerful influences but to minimize the damage and mitigate the consequences. Positively and ideally, community workers are striving for a society which is urbanized, bureaucratized and industrialized but at the same time encourages humanity and fellowship.

Additional reasons

To complete the picture we need to look briefly at a few further reasons for the present interest in community work. They do not receive the universal recognition which is accorded to those we have just considered. Also, as will appear, they are associated with the 'Big Three' but have enough distinctiveness to warrant separate mention.

Mass media of communication particularly television and radio

The mounting influence of, reliance upon and actual coverage by television and radio has affected community development in two complementary approaches. In many ways it has strengthened the demands for popular participation in the affairs of the nation since, through its semi-independent status, it has itself often criticized the 'Establishment': and in so doing it has both focused the latent radical criticism in our society and reinforced it. The impact of the programme *That Was The Week That Was* is only one of many possible examples. It first went out in November 1962. 'The novelty was its catholic audacity. It mocked everybody, not just the traditionally safe targets that do not sue, such as British Rail and the Post Office. It brought the television equivalent of the newspaper cartoon to bear on anyone who roused its sense of mockery. . . . It sought to carry controversy into all areas where argument was possible.'[21] It was a licence for the public to express their views about, and laugh at, every accepted authority in the land. But the public response was at least as significant as the fact and content of the programme. 'Aimed at an irreverent minority it was cast as a late show for Saturday nights, but within a few weeks it was reaching a regular audience of ten millions and had become the most talked about television programme in the world' (p. 215). We are suggesting that the meaning of these and similar events for community development is that they show, among other things, that television can express some of the frustrations of a people who are no longer prepared to accept unquestioningly the rule of their leaders. But if the appositeness of this illustration is not acceptable, there are plenty more, though less spectacular illustrations from present practice. On both sound and vision, talk-in programmes are becoming commonplace: they offer members of the public opportunities to participate in public discussion of vital issues by the use of the telephone. Additionally, there are certainly some of the twenty BBC local radio stations who see their primary function as being to provide community groups with the chance to use air-time to express their views, assisted and guided by professional producers and technicians.

Conversely, the power of the mass media is regarded as a threat and a hindrance by those who have set their hopes on community development. For clearly, despite the recent changes, only a few hands control the levers of power: there are covert mechanisms of 'Establishment' power: by no stretch of imagination can it be called 'the voice of the people'. It is a complex matter and perhaps light will be shed by the discussion which will precede the negotiations for the renewal of the charter in 1976. Much future controversy lies here and we have had a strong foretaste of it already.

An example occurred in January 1972 when a television programme about Northern Ireland was arranged—*The Question of Ulster—An Enquiry into the Future*. Lord Devlin was invited to chair the discussion and the rival factions, excluding the IRA, were to take part. The Home Secretary, Mr Maudling, objected to the programme on the grounds that it was inflammatory and irresponsible. In the end it was broadcast.

Growth of the social sciences

Science seeks the acquisition of knowledge, education aims at its dissemination. In both these spheres the social sciences have been active in this century. The researches of psychologists and sociologists have led to a stronger emphasis on the social basis of personality. It has come to be felt more and more that men and women are to be understood only in terms of their environment. The old faculty psychology has given way to *gestalt* interpretations and field theories. One germane consequence is the common practice today of understanding human behaviour causally rather than morally. We are more inclined to ask what went wrong for a criminal rather than what he did wrong.

This perspective has had wide influence. It is the custom of reactionaries to blame students' revolt at universities in large measure on the sociology department and to point to the fact that students from the faculty are often most active in any disturbance.

They are right to the extent that students within this academic discipline are likely to be the first to be aware of the causal perspective on human behaviour and to locate the fault in society rather than in the individual. But the view is by no means restricted to those who benefit by higher education. The generally higher standards of education have something to do with its wider acceptance. But it represents a new climate of opinion. 'What chance did he have?' people will say about anybody who has fallen short of society's expectation. They are acutely aware that poverty, bad housing and bad education lie behind deviance.

For community development, two consequences follow. First there is, as we have seen in the last section, a scepticism about all forms of authority, a scepticism which moves between the healthy and the irresponsible. Every ideology, it is felt, is a conspiracy. All authority figures are seeking their own advantage. All expressions of social control are a confidence trick. The logical result of this temper is pressure to spread power more widely. The second pertinent consequence is to prompt community caring, compassion and responsibility. In former times if a man and his family were suffering hardship and misfortune the common response would be, 'Why doesn't he do something about it?' Today the same circumstances evoke the response, 'Why doesn't society do something about it?'

Future under-employment in Britain

Relatively few advocates press the argument which arises from increasing leisure. Advances in automation, and general changes in industrial processes and economic life, indicate that people will be less likely in the future to work a forty-hour week for forty years. We may expect that many measures will be adopted to recognize these circumstances, things like longer full-time schooling and earlier retirement. The TUC has already called for a four-day working week though to be truthful it is not one of their most insistent demands. Altogether the future appears to hold the prospect of much more leisure for the masses. The prospect terrifies those who are used to thinking that a full day's work alone represents honesty and self-respect. We have already begun to talk about the problems of leisure and the paradox of this phrase eludes us. Of course the purveyors of commercial entertainment are not displeased. But there are others who see the situation in terms also of an expansion of educational opportunities, particularly for adults: indeed the notion is catching on that education is properly a lifetime's commitment. It is not that passive and superficial forms of entertainment are thought of as necessarily wrong. But it is felt that there will have to be many more opportunities in the future for people to develop their creative gifts and continue learning and acquire excellencies which continually challenge and fulfil them. The problem of leisure is far more than the task of filling in empty hours with harmless pastimes. Those who have ceased to be wage-slaves should not be restricted to becoming slaves of bad art and trivia and titillation. This involves an adult education programme which can help people to find what they are good at among a range of activities which includes drama, literature, music, cookery, gardening and a thousand others. But they should not exclude community service and community participation both of which offer the chance to be active in a human and fulfilling way. Voluntary service is already for many a major leisure-time activity. Participation in public affairs will be an increasing possibility for those from whose brows has been lifted the threat of economic insecurity and who have been taught to expect that they should participate.

Reactions against individualism

The fashions of thinking and feeling in modern societies swing between a stress on the individual and on the society. And of course both stresses will be represented in the same society and will be supported by conflicting voices. Most philosophies and psychological systems can be categorized on this system. Some thinkers, like Freud, depict the individual as restricted by his society: others see that the only hope of individuals is their relationship to the corporate whole. Schopenhauer, in his famous fable of the hedgehogs, saw individuals as needing the same social contacts which wounded them. In sociology too a similar pattern may be traced. Weber is interested in the meaning which men impose on their social circumstances: Durkheim is more concerned with the reality of society which confronts the individual.

More germane to our theme is the fact that the fashion of public opinion at any one time tends to express a popular prejudice in favour of the individual or the society as the focus of attention and value. For various reasons, in post-war Britain there has been a swing towards individualism. A significant catch-phrase of the day is 'doing your own thing'. But now there are signs that among some groups, especially of young people, there is a desire to redress the balance somewhat by a renewal of corporate experience. We can see this in the various communes, in the growth of 'contact' groups, in many of the manifestations of religious revivalism on both sides of the Atlantic.

If it is true that a significant number of the citizens are becoming dissatisfied with a strong emphasis on individualism, this sentiment could well be one of the driving forces behind the present enthusiasm for community work, of which one of the aims is to rediscover human solidarity.

Critics of the notion

We cannot fairly exclude from our consideration a brief mention of those, who to say the least, would approach the subject with modified rapture. There are those who think the whole notion is misconceived and disagree with the primary motive of community development. They are usually found to be making what in general terms might be called a Marxist approach. They suspect that support for the method is likely to come from those who see their positions of power and wealth threatened and judge this as the only means of staving off the evil day when 'the expropriators are expropriated'. Flagging institutions like the church, features of a capitalist society, can be expected to seize upon the idea with enthusiasm since it gives them a new role when they have ceased to be relevant. These critics point to the significance of the fact that community work is problem-orientated where the problems— such as delinquency—are as defined by capitalism. Moreover, they argue that it cannot be serious and sincere in its objectives of radical social change since it rarely comes to grips with the existing structures of political power and economic wealth. So to them it is a defence mechanism, a substitute for the required revolution, a subtle form of social control at a time when the old crude forms are no longer acceptable. It is an ideology of equality in an affluent society where the problem of poverty remains untouched,

Many critics who would not want to make this root-and-branch objection, or any from a Marxist position, would still approach the whole subject with a marked lack of enthusiasm. It does not, in their view, reckon seriously with the privatism and the apathy about public affairs which characterizes many of the people in this country. Outside their own family affairs, and aside from matters which touch them closely, it is said that the vast majority do not want to participate in and be involved with community issues.

There is some support for this discouraging judgment in the results of many community work projects. John Spencer's account of work on certain British council estates[22] may be regarded as typical of many others. Measurable results were small. A youth club, a crèche and an adventure playground were all seriously disappointing. Far from welcoming the opportunities for involvement people were inclined to say 'Why pick on me?'

Elsewhere, of course, results have been more encouraging. But in answer to the question 'How far has community action got in Britain?' Ann Lapping answered 'nowhere'.[23]

Present view

There is considerable force in every one of these objections, but in our view, even cumulatively they do not represent a sufficient denial of the hope that lies in community development.

Accounts of the later projects suggest an increase in the gains for community education, and perhaps we are now reaching the phase where we are profiting by earlier failures.

In any case, the value of the notion is not to be judged solely on the pragmatic considerations of projects attempted, so far. (It is very difficult to invent tangible criteria.) The intrinsic merit of the idea has also to be taken into account. As a last defence we might even be prepared to argue that sometimes it may be better to fail in attempting the right task than to succeed in the wrong task.

Moreover, whilst it is undoubtedly true that Marxism has yielded indispensable insight into human behaviour and societal structures, we do not feel that unaided and unmodified it gives anything like complete or sufficient account of social action. So we do not feel that at the start of the journey we have to make a positive choice between two gates marked respectively, 'Evolution' and 'Revolution'.

Of course we are all capable of using community development as a defence mechanism just as we are capable of using anything else for egotistical purposes. But our admittedly value-loaded judgment is that in this imperfect world we have to accept each other's best intentions and rely on them, whilst we know that unconsciously they will be affected by self-seeking and anxiety.

It is not ours to fancy what were fair, providing it could be, but to start with the world as it is.

6 The values of community work

Disagreements about values

When men argue they are liable to disagree on several grounds. They may be working with opposing sets of facts and no agreement can be reached until the truth of the matter has been established. Both sets of evidence cannot be correct. Or there may be an obvious flaw in the reasoning processes of one of the participants which can be pointed out. But a commoner and more difficult source of conflict is due to a clash in values. The evidence may be agreed and the reasoning flawless but the disputation continues because each side has a different interpretation of the matter under examination. Of course this is far more likely to occur when the subject is philosophical, for example religious or political, but the situation as described is by no means confined to these subjects. Much discussion is both vitiated and enriched by the prejudices and convictions of those taking part. This discounts a naïve expectation in some quarters that all the differences between individuals and groups can be settled by a conference or a 'get-together'. It overlooks the reality that all of us interpret phenomena in the light of an inbuilt value-system which is a product of our individual development and social experience. And most of us are capable of 'cooking the evidence' in the light of our conviction that some things are better than others without further proof. There is no disputing tastes.

In groups that meet for the purposes of popular education, the question may arise, Why do clever people disagree profoundly on fundamental issues? Why is Professor Mandarin a religious believer and a Conservative whilst the equally erudite Professor Knowall is an atheist and a Communist? Ordinary people feel sometimes that they would like to hand over to outstanding authorities decisions about major issues which affect their lives. But on every one of these major issues equally competent authorities can be quoted on opposite sides of the fence. Clearly they are bringing personal and emotional elements into their conclusions. It could be that on closer examination Professor Mandarin turns out to be one whose lifelong outlook has been deeply affected by a pious and adored father, whereas Professor Knowall is compensating for a lack of social feeling.

Discussions with colleagues and students seem often to uncover a major obstacle to full recognition of the part played in argument, enquiry and interaction by subjective and evaluative constituents. It is the well-known and quite proper insistence that the social scientist is 'value-free',[1] concerned to describe what is rather than what ought to be, as interested in the activities of the criminal as in efforts to reform him. This must be part of the ethos of the profession since the social scientist who ceases to be non-judgmental in his enquiries allows his vision to be clouded. But many people press the insistence to unrealistic and illegitimate extremes. They may be found, for example, inferring that this means there are no values. Here they have strayed, without (perhaps) noticing, across an academic frontier into the realms of philosophy where the social scientist as such has no sovereign right to pronounce. (The whole issue is the subject of our next chapter.) A further misunderstanding arises when we confuse the social thinker or theorist with the social worker. Earlier it was our contention that though the former is required to be 'value-free', the latter cannot afford that luxury. He too is chastened by professional standards in this matter, but daily decisions are forced upon him where the only guiding light is a value system. Finally, in all kindness, one wishes to ask how 'value-free' in fact social scientists are. Are we not talking here about an aspiration rather than an achievement? And an aspiration that must often be restricted to their conscious choices and often takes little account of their unconscious preferences. They are men of the same clay as the rest of us, what they see is determined partly by what they are, their differences cannot always be explained by different evidence or the unemotional conflict of judgment. One of their favourite themes is 'the sociology of knowledge' which is an insight that knowledge varies with the environment, that the doctrines men defend are not unrelated to the satisfaction of their own needs. It is a view not without confirmation in the affairs of men. But one sometimes finds sociologists who refuse to drink their own medicine. 'The sociology of knowledge' applies also to our knowledge of society: the conclusions of sociologists are affected by their environment. One big divide, for example, is between those who are disposed to seek stability in society and those whose desires are in the direction of change and revolution.

'Values' play a prominent part in the real world, which is not always the same as the imaginary world of some social theorists. This is often illustrated in common speech. 'I value your friend-ship' we say in a sentimental moment. 'There are things that matter to me more than money or position' wrote a young business-man refusing to accept promotion and electing to stay in a village. 'Well, I am sorry, I don't see it like that' can be the conclusion of an argument where we recognize that the dialectic is unfavourable.

Most human behaviour is guided by value assumptions and follows the pattern of the brave opening words of the American Declaration of Independance (4 July 1776): 'We hold these truths to be self-evident. . . .' Like the American Founding Fathers we may not stop to enquire just how self-evident the truths are.

We have devoted attention to this point for a practical reason. One is constantly encountering community workers who want to insist that they are 'value-free' and 'non-judgmental'. They are saying something here that is important both for us and for them. But it is hard to suppress the conviction that many of them need to think more carefully about the meaning of this statement and to express that meaning more accurately. Certainly—as we shall presently see—those who have thought and written on the community development process have been ready to give more prominence to the underlying value assumptions.

The point seems clear enough. What people will seek for in their community bears a direct relation to their total outlook on life, though it is also true that their social circumstances in a community will also affect their total outlook on life. Stein has frank comments to make on the style of life of many suburbanites on the American continent.[2]

No one is surprised to discover that businessmen treat each other in impersonal and manipulative terms; but surely it should be cause for some dismay to find it habitual . . . that mothers regard suburban children as 'cases' the moment they lag behind the highly formalized routine accomplishments of their peers, or, still worse, show signs of distinctive individuality.

Can it be denied that one of the driving forces behind these unfortunate attitudes is a philosophy of 'other-directedness', the belief that conformity and the approval of one's fellows is the supreme good to be sought?

The meaning of 'values'

'Values' is an ambiguous term: its present use should be made clear.

There is the familiar distinction in the use of the term depending on whether we are talking from a sociological or a philosophical point of view. In the former case, we are merely describing what is without any attempt to pronounce on the validity or worth of what we observe. As human beings we may deplore the fact that many white people in the deep south of the USA consider themselves inherently superior to black people: but despite our disapproval we have still to recognize a standard which guides the social behaviour of many thousands of people in Alabama, Georgia and Tennessee. Philosophy is concerned with the status of values though its answers differ all the way from the eternal status given to them in Platonism to the dismissal of all discussion of values as meaningless and impossible.

In this chapter we are concerned with values in the first, socio-logical, sense as part of a social reality, as they exist in the experience of those who in the broadest sense are community workers. What are the motivations of these people? Given the traditional circumstances conducive to joint action, what are the value-systems prompting them to direct, and often sustained and costly, involvement? Thinking of human beings living together in society, what features of their association do they deem to be better than others, whether these assumptions be latent or manifest?

To expand on a previous point, the necessary presence of such value-assumptions is widely recognized by those—the social philosophers and 'architects' of community development—who have written on our subject. The statements of the Gulbenkian report[3] can be accepted as characteristic.

Community work is rooted in certain beliefs which derive from our culture and society and are shared with a number of helping professions and reforming activities. Basically they are concerned with ideas about human worth and betterment. Different people express them in different ways and with varying emphases, but at a broad level of generality or vagueness there is considerable overlap.

Many of the best-known investigators researching the communities have been avowedly so far concerned with human values that, in a slightly teasing passage, Colin Bell and Howard Newby accuse them of halting the growth of theoretical concepts.[4]

Below the surface of many community studies lurk value judgements, of varying degrees of explicitness. . . . With a distaste that shouts from the page, Vidich and his two colleagues complain that 'the development of abstract concepts, complex indices and statistical devices in the more scientific methodologies and the use of highly structured research instruments has little direct knowledge of the social world they are supposed to survey'.

What are these values?

It would be possible to provide general answers that are frequently noted for their idealism rather than their precision. In this setting, Sir Oliver Frank's definition of democracy as deriving from three basic ideas would serve: 'the value of the individual human personality, a real sense of belonging, and the basic like-mindedness which is the root of democratic life'.[5] But enlightening and inspiring as that may be for some, it is not specific enough for our purpose.

Obviously in this matter community workers occupy large areas of common ground with members of other helping professions: and notably with other types of social workers. There is of course a similarity between the objectives of social work methods whether they are concerned with individuals, groups or neighbourhoods. They share an ethos. They are concerned to remove hindrances to the full use of human resources. But it is possible to overemphasize the similarities and blur the distinctions. Their emphasis and focus of attention and methods are often different. Similarly, the values of a teacher are close relatives of those of the community worker. Ottaway has provided the three principles

H

which lie behind the educational system of a democracy. '(i) All people are in some sense equal, (ii) All people have certain essential freedoms, (iii) Government by consent.'[6] But again, despite much common ground, one set will not suffice for both teachers and community workers.

Our aim is to provide a list which is general enough to hope to secure the support of the vast majority of workers and thinkers in our field, yet to be specific enough to highlight features which receive special prominence in community work.

As to the first, there are those who despair of ever finding a consensus about values among community workers. When we compare them as individuals we find they often come from contrasted backgrounds, look at the social scene in different terms and often argue about objectives. But on closer scrutiny they may be found to be not at odds about the general aims, ends and values but about one or more of four related matters. (1) How they express their values. (2) How these values apply to particular situations. (3) The order of priority for various values. (4) The reasons or sanctions which in each case lie behind those values. These dissonances still contain, of course, the possibility of large conflict but they may not preclude a general statement.

As to the specific features of our ethos, these will be found to lie in the stress upon co-operative processes as being important alike for the individual and his society. Any list should make this clear. They see the whole society as both the protector and the workshop, offering support and fulfilment for the individual, dealing in the twin realities of provision and participation.

In this vein, the Gulbenkian report treats the matter in summarizing the values thus:[7]

i   That a democratic society exists to enable all its citizens to develop their various talents and interests to the fullest possible extent. . . .

ii That much of the individual's capacity for growth and development depends on his active association with his fellows in a number of different groups. . . .

iii That respect for another individual must include respect for his beliefs, his ability to reach decisions and to build his own life. . . .

iv That society thrives on the interplay between leadership, organization and freedom, though few can suggest what the right balance is between organization from above and development from below. . . .

Our own list is at once more detailed and uses an inductive approach in that it relies upon the recorded encounters of many workers. The value system can be represented by a constellation with five stars each of which is represented by a proposition and one or more of which will be present in the minds of the operatives. This remains impressionistic but we would expect them to score highly on a factoral testing of the following attitudes.

Each individual is important   Ronald Blythe in his portrait of an English village[8] has provided unforgettable pictures of the serf-like position of servants on large estates during this century.

I went to Lordship's when I was fourteen and stayed for fourteen years. . . . It was a frightening experience for a boy. Lord and Ladyship were very, very Victorian and very domineering. It was 'swing your arms' every time they saw us. Ladyship would appear suddenly from nowhere when one of us boys were walking off to fetch something. 'Swing your arms' she would shout. We wore green baize aprons and collars and ties, no matter how hot it was, and whatever we had to do had to be done on the dot. . . . We must never be seen from the house: it was forbidden. And if people were sitting on the terrace or the lawn, and you had a great barrow-load of weeds, you might have to push it as much as a mile to keep out of view. . . . It was terrible. You felt like somebody with a disease. . . . We had to creep in early in the morning before breakfast and replace great banks of flowers in the main room. Lord and Ladyship must never hear or see you doing it. . . . Servants were just part of the machinery of the big house and people don't thank machines, they just keep them trim and working. . . . Ladyship drove about the grounds in a motor-chair and would have run us over rather than have to say 'Get out of the way'.

Such élitism is anathema today for public opinion but the strongest reactions are likely to come from community workers whose rationale is the high and equal worth of human beings. This is expressed in and fed by their daily encounters, where, whatever the stress on corporate action, they spend a major portion of their time encouraging individuals and helping them with their personal problems of felt inadequacy and lack of self-confidence. They subscribe to the idea, though many of them would be unhappy with the wording, expressed by Henri Bergson: 'Democracy is evangelical in essence. . . . Its motive power is love.'

Not surprisingly in view of the historical background, the most unashamedly frank admissions of this human evaluation are found in the related areas of struggles against race and colour discrimination and work in developing countries. As to the first, one of the haunting pictures of the twentieth century is the memory of Martin Luther King, shortly before his death, walking in a procession where his coloured compatriots carried banners proclaiming 'We are men'. On the second there is, we may suspect, a long history of people in poor countries who meet the western advisers come with the best intentions to do them good, but revealed by time to lack an inner respect for the people among whom they work. Typical is a comment from a book which records sympathetically many attempts of the rich nations to help the poorer nations.[9]

> One of the most widely accepted principles of community development is that activities should be based upon 'the felt needs' of the people concerned. The universality of agreement on this point in theory is matched only by the infrequency with which it is truly applied in practice. It is probable, however, that there is something more fundamental than the 'felt needs' concept. The more fundamental concept is that of respect for people, the recognition of their dignity and potentiality. The recognition of 'felt needs' is only one of the consequences of this basic consideration of respect for people.

The duty of a democratic society is to care for the welfare and development of individual citizens This ethos is pushed to the point where the measure of a state is not in its wealth but in how the wealth is used and distributed: not in its martial glory or overseas possessions but in its welfare and educational programmes. And nowhere is the criterion applied more strictly than in its application to the care devoted to the handicapped, underprivileged and 'economically unprofitable'.

To repeat a point previously made—if we read today, in history books or novels, accounts of Victorian individualism, we realize how large is the change in the mental climate. Then a man was expected to look after himself and his family, today the State is expected to care for him and them. It is often said that this is only a consciously accepted norm, that at unconscious levels, public opinion still expects the poor to heal themselves of their poverty. Though that were true, the change remains impressive as appears when we meet a traditionalist who will unashamedly defend the old approaches. Some few years ago, I had lunch with a professor on an American college campus. He was a delightful companion, humane, urbane, civilized and well-versed in his subject. But on one subject he seemed to me to be not quite sane and certainly he could not discuss it dispassionately. He regarded every act of government intervention to help the poor, unemployed, sick and old as communism. America had become the richest nation on earth through the rugged individualism which had developed in a society where every man was left, more or less, to stand on his own feet. The American way of life was undermined, he thought, by every attempt to create a welfare society. Perhaps one needs to confront its opposite to appreciate how widespread in this country is the expressed conviction about community care: but it is most marked amongst community workers. They are driven by a demand for social justice. They insist that technological, industrial and economic programmes have to be tested for their social and human consequences.

Along with this, under pressure from the demands of the situation, there has arisen the insistence on the importance of a holistic approach to the human problems in a society. Fragmentation of effort can meet one need whilst it makes another more acute or even creates new needs that cannot be satisfied. It is true that a holistic approach often painfully exposes the nature of priority choices but it is usually better to plan for the whole. I recall visiting the chief municipal planner in that city of poignant human deprivation—Calcutta. He greeted me with the words 'You have come to a dying city'. After outlining the major problems—signs of which had been all too evident to me on my brief visit—he went on:

The real problem is where to begin. Don't say birth control.
Many of our women could not read the instructions. Is it
primary education? The most practical thing to help the
people of Calcutta would be to build another bridge over the
River Hooghly which runs through the centre. There is only
one bridge for thirteen million people. Another bridge would
relieve the congestion and improve the whole life of the
people.

Right or wrong, it was a decision he had taken in the light of his
knowledge of the total needs of the population.

Freedom is a goal to be sought   They wish to increase the opportunities for the citizen to share in decisions which affect the whole
society. Democracy to them is more than the use of the ballot-box.
That provision can exist side by side with enervating, frustrating
and callous bureaucracy. They realize that increased participation
will bring unrest, strife and uncertainty, but they think that on the
grounds of human dignity, it is, even so, to be preferred to an
oligarchy. They judge that a troubled free man has the advantage
of a contented slave. Modern community workers are not disposed
to look for Biblical parables of their situation but should they ever
care to turn up the passages they will find the children of Israel,
after their escape from Egypt, complaining of the perplexities of
their emancipation. 'Would God we had died in the land of
Egypt' or, 'would God we had died in this wilderness'.[10] And they
will find Moses constantly bracing them to the recognition of the
intrinsic merit of freedom by confronting them with the stark
choice of returning to bondage. 'But as for you, turn and take your
journey into the wilderness by way of the Red Sea.'[11]

*Democracy and participation are ultimately to be preferred on the
grounds of efficiency, as well as for their humanity*   This is the value
which has received most punishment from the critics, chiefly on
the grounds that it rests on naïve and even sentimental
assumptions. The mass of the people, we are told, do not want to
take part in public affairs: they merely want to be left alone to
pursue their own interests and affairs of the family. Bracey[12] has
pointed to an additional factor in the British tradition, namely, the
tendency to look to the aristocracy for leadership and public

service. But the general charge is that these enthusiasts have overestimated the strength of communal feeling among the population and underestimated the strength of egotistical drives. Their optimism is thought to ascribe more credit to their hearts than to their heads.

Public opinion veers between the extremes of utopianism and despair, and at any one time contains elements of both. It must be admitted that the philosophy of community work errs if at all on the side of optimism. The present purpose is not to evaluate these hypotheses but we ought to say what we think they are and when they are stated they appear to represent great hopes.

Ideally, community development aims to be not just a taming of the masses but wants to release emotional forces of goodwill and co-operation which it believes are locked up inside ordinary people. To a degree it rests upon a belief in the perfectability of human nature. It answers charges of widespread apathy about public affairs with the comment that the citizens have never before had the opportunities of power and responsibility. When these are available there will be a significant response. Again, society itself is made the scapegoat for individual lack of responsibility.[13]

Part of the problem of dealing with such behaviour lies in the attitude of those in power—political, economic or social—who work within the limits of their own rather rigid ideas about society, which may have roots in the past and may not be by any means necessarily valid in the light of accurate contemporary analysis of the facts. . . . What goes wrong may partly originate in what organized society does to people.

We find these brave and hopeful statements scattered throughout the literature on the subject. 'The worker must proceed on the assumption that constructive forces of goodwill and co-operation exist and that it is his task to release them.'[14] 'Worst of all, a community developer may too believe that people of a certain category are condemned to permanent inferiority. If so, he will forfeit his role of encourager.'[15] The same authority, characteristic of his kind, argues that many projects have already demonstrated that the assumptions about human nature which would discourage community processes are invalid.[16] Nor is he by any means alone in concluding that societies contain an untapped source of leadership material among the masses of the population.[17] We are presented not merely with an optimism about Man who is now seen as having climbed into the saddle of power: we are shown an optimism about men who can become efficient in gaining control over local aspects of a frustrating and changing world.

Community development is usually found to rest on a deep conviction that given a chance it will work. Basic human goodness and the immense possibilities of individuals guarantee this. Moreover, if we want a decent society, nothing else will work. That is the common commitment.

Co-operation and fellowship are better than isolation This is another assumption, interwoven with the thinking and practice of community workers, which can be regarded apart from any concrete results which follow from the projects. It is thought to be good that men should co-operate whatever the result of their association. The personal relationships which result are a valuable bonus, almost, some are inclined to think, a sufficient end in themselves. Many of the approaches rest on an oft-repeated quotation from John Donne: 'No man is an Island, entire of itself.' The vast majority of men, it is felt, will discover their humanity, not in the creation of private or even family worlds, but in active association with their fellows.

It is idle for us to speculate overmuch on why this emphasis receives strong support at the present time. We have already suggested that the present enthusiasm for community may represent a swing of the pendulum away from the individualism of our epoch. Another insight is also persuasive. The ancient faiths which made men kin have lost their hold and perhaps substitutes have to be found which attempt to preserve our like-mindedness and save us from feeling alone in a world which often seems hostile to our best hopes. But whatever its source, the conviction that we need to be in active association with our fellows will be found to be common amongst workers and thinkers in this field.

The reluctance to discuss values

There are several reasons why workers are shy of the kind of discussion we are engaged in. Some of the reasons have impressive validity and considerable force. Briefly, we may say that thinking in this regard is influenced by a history of social and educational work which from a modern perspective holds unsatisfactory features. In addition, we are operating in an intellectual climate which favours relativism in the conceptualization of moral and spiritual values. We are inclined to think that they come not 'from above' but from within and from social life. These two points will be examined in detail.

Occasionally in the books that have been written on this subject we come across open and avowed commitments to a set of values.[18]

The question of respect for domestic property leads to that of respect for public property, and therefore, implicitly, to the maintenance of public order and the establishment of a high public morale. In some parts of the country, and more particularly in some of the central urban areas, there is long-standing resistance to the police and mistrust of them may remain even where a new function, such as the juvenile liaison schemes, has permitted a respect for certain aspects of police work. It is for this reason that all social agencies should direct some of their attention to the matter of civic responsibility, if only at the level of public order. The lead given from the pulpit and in the school assembly needs to be followed up in the home, the youth club, the pub and the cinema.

There are advocates of social change who contend that the troubles of our time are so great that only revolutionary changes to problems will suffice. And they add that community activities should fit into some such revolution. . . . Many proposers of community change convince themselves of their own importance by talking about revolution. . . . Such talk tells more of a desire for sensationalism than of their determination to solve great problems in a fundamental way. . . . A contrast is important at this point between [the encourager's] role and that of the dead-in-earnest advocates of needed social change. These necessary people (who are often willing to become martyrs in the cause of votes, registration of the underprivileged, or in opposition to war, or in elimination of racial discrimination) are to be admired. Theirs is, however, a determinedly devoted and humourless role.

Such utterances are likely to draw strong expressions of dissent particularly from young community workers, as the writer knows from not a few discussions. 'Bourgeois' and 'reactionary' are among the politer adjectives which are used on these occasions.

One large factor is the wider distribution of psychological and sociological knowledge. A popular realization that many of our moral insights are the result of social conditioning has eroded the base of many authoritarian value systems. What a man believes to be right or wrong will have much to do with the culture in which he has been brought up, the class to which he belongs and the preference of his parents. The non-academic way of putting the matter is in the sort of phrase which is often inserted into informal arguments. 'You only say that because of the way you were brought up.' One man will never fully enjoy recreation on Sunday, because, whatever his reason tells him today, he is still emotionally influenced by the Sabbatarian strictness of his parents during his earliest and most impressionable years. There are few virtues in any one culture which have not been regarded as vices elsewhere. If our value systems are socially provided and socially defined why then do we presume them to have universal validity, particularly for people with very different social and personal experiences from our own? W. B. Yeats is credited with the expression, 'People are responsible for their opinions but Providence is responsible for their morals'.[19] But educated modern man finds it increasingly hard to distinguish between the two.

It follows that community workers—and social workers generally as well as educationalists to a lesser degree—feel they must constantly be on guard against projecting their moral values and expectations on to others. The vulnerability is most obviously present, and often in a dramatic and spectacular form, in community work, in what are euphemistically called developing countries: all this is simply because the worker has most frequently been brought up in American or European society from which he brings his standards. Confronted by alien standards of hygiene, structures of power and privilege, systems of polygamy, say, and the persistence of superstitions, try as he will, he may be hard put not to recoil with dislike or even abhorrence. He may fail to show how 'right' and inevitable these things are for the person concerned since they are functional and form part of a social system. One quotation will suffice since it is not only a summary of many illustrations but also sounds a warning note for those who have a worthy concern to raise the material standards of life in poorer countries.[20]

The expert sees the material setting of Asian life, often so reduced to the bare essentials of living that it appears to him to be totally lacking in all that he thinks makes life worthwhile. What he fails to see is that this is not a case of failure to achieve material rewards but a dedicated and idealistic process of voluntarily 'giving up', through control, abstinence, penance and sacrifice. Many in Asia believe, in a simple and direct way, that progress is to be measured in terms of the purification of the spirit of man.

Coming nearer home we find that community workers feel they are liable in particular to one form of 'value-projection'. The majority of them come from middle-class backgrounds and their constituencies are nearly always in working-class areas. They suspect themselves of tendencies to bourgeois perspectives and judgments which will certainly be inappropriate for their clientele. So we often find them struggling to accept language, leisure-time habits and family relationships—among other realities—which are alien to their nurture.

Much space has been devoted to pointing out the same danger for the teaching profession, though social workers often feel that teachers are not so likely to be sensitive to the peril or introspective about their authority. According to Bernstein, even the language of education is middle-class.[21] A summary of Jackson and Marsden's conclusions[22] might well be that not only is the school largely middle class in ethos but that teachers are either drawn from the middle class or usually become bourgeois in outlook after joining the profession. Lawrence Stenhouse is one of the writers on education who has shown himself sensitive to the dilemma and the opportunity.[23]

The formal teacher generally finds support for his values in a social 'establishment', which embodies the approved values of the society at large. . . . He tends either to be conservative in standards, attempting to transmit received values to a new generation, or to try at least to encourage innovation only within a rather close framework such as the established methods of science or recognized literary forms. . . . By contrast, teachers who have been influenced by the progressive movement in education tend to turn for their standards to other teachers or to artists and innovators.

Social workers of all kinds are likely to show themselves more aware of the conflict though they are by no means always successful in its resolution. It can be painful even to watch. They want, on the one hand, to be non-judgmental so they will not lose touch with their clients or patronize or control them. But on the other they wish not to damage their own integrity by betraying those values, which, wherever they may have acquired them, are now a part of themselves. Brought up to respect personal property, the worker may have to accept a lot of petty pilfering among those who lacked the same indoctrination. At first, he may wince at the use of language which is common currency among his new colleagues, though this feature of the enterprise is markedly less prominent since the use of 'language' has stepped across the barriers. One detached youth worker describes how he was willing to attend a wild party at the home of a girl whose parents were on holiday but he clearly disapproved of some promiscuous sexual activity which was associated with these parties.[24]

A further refinement of this self-examination occurs when the worker accuses himself of insisting upon the class symbols of his ethical standards. Thus not to swear in the presence of ladies may be for some a bourgeois recognition of the fact that it is, after all, the women who bear the heavier burdens of life. Working-class people may not follow this mode but they may have other symbols of chivalrous recognition. Politeness is simply a way of showing consideration for others but its ritualized expressions will vary from place to place and between class and class.

In any of these senses, to impose one's values on the clients is for social workers the sin against the Holy Ghost, the denial of the right of self-determination and a failure to accept people as they are.

It has to be remembered that the social workers of today are the inheritors of a tradition which stretches back at least as far as the last century. A balanced view, content to be guided by historical perspective, would concede that there were pleasing features of these early attempts of benefactors to help the less fortunate victims of an industrial society. But it was not unmixed altruism and the work contained features which make it suitable for use as a horrible example today. It was paternalistic, undertaken by people who were sure that they knew what was good for others. It was an aspect of social control designed partly to keep the masses from causing too much trouble. It was firmly on the side of the establishment and did not propose to question the existing structures of power or the present distribution of wealth. It was prone to preaching. And it was all of these things because for the most part the people who operated it were, despite their compassion, ideologically cocksure: they rarely stopped to question whether the morality they preached contained disguised elements of protection for their class interests: they had God on their side.

Social work sprang from such a matrix and in this century it has staged a rebellion against mother.

The value of discussing values

There is merit in the reluctance of community workers to dwell on the values which lie behind their efforts: for one thing it is an insistence on action after a long period of talk. But the reluctance can represent loss as well as gain.

For it can inhibit that self-awareness which all 'in the trade' would agree is a *sine qua non* of success. To work with unacknowledged motives can be a loss of power and may even result in self-deception. Flexibility may also be sacrificed. The ancient Greek adage 'Know thyself: accept thyself: be thyself' applies to modern social workers. Paul Halmos has demonstrated[25] that social workers with a concern to be 'scientific, objective and professional' are often operating with unacknowledged value structures. Hence they often use the disguised language of love and even of theology. From one point of view this could be an attractive form of 'hypocrisy', claiming to care less than you do. But from another perspective it can be stated that all lack of self-awareness represents a flight from reality. Everything has to be brought into the open for effectiveness.

This mode of realism pays dividends in three areas. First, for the worker himself: all illusions about one's self are a source of weakness, wastage of psychic power and a strain. Part of the energy needed for the work is diverted into maintaining the fiction. Second, with colleagues: mutual support and under-standing, as well as co-operation in the field, are facilitated by the willingness to expose the value assumptions on which we are working. Third, with lay participants from the community: one aspect of our work is to appeal to the idealism which we believe often lies dormant in the minds of the citizens. It would be altogether too cynical to conclude that members of the public can only and always be appealed to in terms of their own self-interest. There have been occasions in our recent national history when thoughtful observers think that politicians have failed precisely because they have not spoken to the moral aspirations of the population. For example, Lord Moran thinks that Winston Churchill misjudged the mood of the British people in 1945 and lost the General Election because he pitched his appeal to their self-interest rather than to their idealism.[26] On a smaller stage, we have to consider whether the community worker can help the people to mobilize their sentiments of idealism unless he has come to terms with his own.

Finally, we have to recognize that behind the value assumptions of most people there is—avowed or unacknowledged—what may be called an 'ideology' in the sense of a total way of looking at life which authorizes their value assumptions. But this consideration brings us to the threshold of our last chapter.

7 The faith of the community worker

It is a characteristic of human beings that they usually act purposefully: they look ahead and do one thing in order that another may eventuate. There are of course great variations among men about how far and how often they look ahead. Economically, we can talk of 'delayed gratification' by which money is not spent to secure immediate satisfactions but used to gain distant objectives. Moral activity suggests that we can modify our conduct in the light of an inner ideal and to secure ethical ends. Events can cause us to change our purpose in the middle of an activity. A parliamentary candidate may enter the local tavern because he genuinely feels in need of refreshment. Once inside he meets a number of customers who evince a disposition to be friendly and listen to him. So he stays, longer than he intended, to indulge in a bit of electioneering and secure a few votes. Animals too, of course, behave purposively, but apparently not with anything approaching the sophistication of human beings.

We have looked at the purposes of community workers: now it is time to enquire carefully what lies behind these purposes.

The meaning of the terms

In the hey-day of the *Brains Trust*, Professor Joad gave to the public a phrase which was so well known that it was appropriated by comedians and cartoonists. 'It depends what you mean by—.' Several times previously in this work we have insisted that our discussion can only proceed if we seek for an agreed meaning of the words we employ and encourage precision in the use of language. Without this attempt we have maintained—perhaps overmuch and to the point of being tiresome—that we cannot know what we are talking about.

Nowhere is this canon so required as in this last section where we are dealing with a highly controversial matter, one which, in fact, often rouses the passions of the most phlegmatic of men. It behoves us, therefore, not merely to tread delicately, but at the beginning to define our terms.

When we talk about 'purpose' we often fall into a common

logical trap. We use the same word to describe psychological realities which are different or only bear a superficial resemblance to each other. And there is no agreed usage so that the same word will represent contrasting mental concepts depending on who is using it.

To illustrate on this matter of purpose, consider the case of the leader of a youth club who is asked a question by a social investigator who has visited the scene of his endeavours, 'What are you trying to do?' Depending on the conversational context and the intenseness of the leader, the answer could be given describing a short-term ('I am collecting names for an outing') or a long-term objective ('Providing opportunities for social education'). We can go further and say that in the latter case, hypothetically, the answer may fall in one of three categories depending on the interpretation given to the question. In the second two we have passed from a bald statement of aims to a description of the underlying reasons for the choice of these tasks. It is in fact in this way that this style of question is frequently understood.

Task: 'I want to have a well-organized club which offers a wide range of activities and opportunities to the members.'

Aims: 'I want to help youngsters in this district to have what is their right.'

Faith: 'I want to do the will of God. I am called to be a youth worker.'

Admittedly the contrasts have been overdrawn in order to make a point. Even the most pious would be unlikely to state his motivations in the hard terms of the third. But it is our contention that under careful scrutiny many community workers are found to have a personal philosophy, a 'world-view'—not necessarily religious of course—which lies behind, validates and supports their efforts. So purpose in our universe of discourse can be understood in one of three main ways: tasks (short-term), values (long-term) and faith (long-term), and on this basis we may construct an unusual continuum.

(mostly short-term)	*Purpose* (long-term)	(mostly long-term)
tasks, achievements, goals	aims, purposes, values	personal philosophy, faith

In this last chapter we concentrate attention on the third category. In a previous section we have identified underlying assumptions to which community workers are prone—that individual citizens have inherent worth and dignity, that given the opportunities they will be disposed to co-operate with their fellows and so on. Sometimes we come across a conviction that these values should have the authority of a world-view. What are their credentials? Is the world as we know it favourable to these hopes? And though, as we shall see, this approach is hotly contested, we discover in practice that the daily endeavours of many community workers are linked with, integrated with, supported and validated by, their own personal philosophy. Behind the value choices usually lie subconscious assumptions about the meaning of life. Many workers, for example, look out upon the scene through Marxist spectacles, consider that the masses are exploited by those who own the means of production and distribution and direct their own efforts to redressing the balance.

The issue has not entirely escaped the attention of those who have explored the depths of a community approach to modern societies. People need to believe in the value of the communities in which they live, the goals they seek, and the satisfactions they receive.[1] Biddle has a passage in which he recognizes the interplay of psychological theories and philosophy resulting in varying approaches in social education and reflecting contrasted conceptions of human nature, its potentialities and destiny.[2]

Various psychological writers have taken mutually contradictory positions with regard to man's potential for improvement. Years ago, the philosopher-psychologist John Dewey challenged the gloomy view of human beings that grew out of earlier theological conclusions about original sin. . . . Later, the behaviourist psychologists, assuming an infinite malleability and leaning heavily upon the work of psychologist Ivan Pavlov, concluded that human beings could be conditioned to a limitless array of behaviour. Their conclusions rest more upon experiments with dogs, rats, monkeys and even pigeons however, than upon experience with people, especially people in the situation of actual living. Having concluded that men and women could be conditioned to almost any behaviour pattern, they were tempted to try to control them. . . . Posed against

this school of thought is the more recently identified
humanistic psychology which accepts human malleability
but points towards generous and prosocial motivations. . . .
All agree upon the necessity for ethical values to guide the
experiments and influences which shall encourage the emergence
of prosocial impulses.

Here the conclusions of social science and the influence of a personal standpoint are inextricably bound together with the traffic of
influence moving both ways. Clearly the methods and approaches
of the grass roots community worker will be affected by a personal
preference for one emphasis or the other. In the end, how we
'see' men decides how we work with them and relate to them.
Thus, personal knowledge of our friends, gathered over a long
harvest, can reveal that beyond all their training and intellectual
commitment, they have a bias to think of individuals in society as
'subjects', 'consumers', 'citizens' or 'souls'.

There is a body of opinion which judges that evil consequences
can follow our failure in all forms of education to grapple with
the questions of man's place and status in the universe. Communities without this form of reference will be more inclined to
seek their own advantage and undertake co-operative effort for
egotistical ends without regard to the welfare of other communities. Community workers, similarly deprived, may, by imperceptible stages, change the focus of attention from improvement in the life of the community to an enhancement in the status
of their own profession. On this view, daily idealism in the work
is likely to be sustained only by the personal world-view or
ideology of the worker.

A further and even more controversial issue arises. Granted the
enduring importance of a personal 'faith' of the worker, does this
have to rest on 'absolute values'? Is religion involved even in the
broadest sense? Will it not be sufficient to demonstrate that an
adequate personal world-view can be provided by 'secular values'
immanent in history, not 'given' by any supernatural agency and
justified simply by the fact that they are required to preserve
civilization in peace, prevent its destruction and encourage everywhere the development of human potentialities? And anyway, is
there any evidence which justifies our reliance upon more than

'secular' hopes? Both sides continue the offensive over this battle-ground.

Is discussion worth while?

This type of discussion is calculated to generate more passion than most others among community workers and social workers and educationists generally. Anybody who has been drawn into the argument may have found himself involved in long disputations that invaded the night. Our own commitment in this matter is not concealed and will escape all efforts to be dispassionate. But we are not about to pronounce on the issue even were this within our competence. All we are concerned to claim at this stage is that here is an argument worth having, where both sides should listen to the other. As in all human disputations, there is often a tendency to dismiss the other side as knaves or fools, or both. But the future prospects of community work appear to depend to a marked degree on the ability of both sides—to be identified roughly with the 'religious' and the 'humanist'—to respect each other and continue to listen to each other.

'Humanists' may find this hard because often they cannot, for the life of them, see the relevance of a 'religious' philosophy for the community worker. They have no need of this 'invisible means of support'. The values involved in the endeavours need no more justification than that, like Mount Everest, 'they are there'. They frankly admit that half of the time they do not know what the other side is talking about.

The evaluation is buttressed by the intellectual companions of community work. Sociology is the closest academic discipline and *per se* it looks at belief systems from an institutional perspective and at individual faith from a functional point of view and as the product of social conditioning. As the role of sociology is to peer behind the scenes, explode the folk myths and to employ a de-bunking motif, it is only to be expected that religious behaviour has not escaped unharmed and unscathed. In many discussions it is a self-evident truth of the 'humanists' that religious faith can be completely explicated in terms of social functionalism and individual determinism. The most they will concede is that a worker's values are internalized, they are part of him and in this sense his private philosophy affects his performance. But this is to be viewed existentially, the rest is incapable of verification. Moreover, his outlook is individual and relative with no authority for others.

But there are controversialists who want to go further than this. Religion (or any other system of absolute values) is for them positively harmful. 'God' is not just a harmless delusion, a private hobby of a few, but a dangerous fantasy. First, it is an instrument by which one section of the human race maintains power over another: every ideology is a conspiracy. Second, it is found in fact to be a divisive force, compelling people to think in exclusive, rather than inclusive, terms, to be particularistic in outlook not universalistic. Then, on the practical level, it is often a restricting force in community work since it operates to persuade those concerned that they know the true needs of those with whom they struggle, making it harder to accept them as they are and discourages the recognition of the right of the citizen to self-determination. Lastly, there are accusations that religion is an influence which operates against true morality since it encourages men to look for deliverance to unseen powers when they should be using their own powers to improve the quality of human living. 'From the moment that the free thinkers began to question the existence of God, the problems of justice became of paramount importance.'[3]

It cannot be denied that each of these propositions could be plentifully illustrated from the history books but what is arguable is whether they represent the whole truth or even whether they are a faithful account of the commonest effects of religious belief in its later forms.

Temperamental differences go some way to explain on which side of the dialectical fence a man will stand. There seem to be 'natural sceptics' as well as 'born believers'. Perhaps everybody coming into the world is either a Platonist—programmed to ponder the meanings which lie behind events—or an Aristotelian —orientated to an analysis of the phenomena which confront us.

Only the unreflective can live with absolute certainties about the ultimate questions. But our sole concern now is to say that at least this is an argument worth having. And as long as a considerable section of the human race feel that they must search for a meaning to life, we cannot dismiss the discussion as irrelevant, particularly if as community workers we are to maintain our proved claim that we seek to begin with the needs of the 'clients'. Whether we decide for or against a religious interpretation, or whether our enquiries prove inconclusive, it can hardly be said that the issues are trivial. We are trying to decide whether to think of man as a moral orphan in an indifferent universe, 'alone on a wide, wide sea'[4] with no answering calls to his cries except from others who are drowning: or whether to think of him as part of a design and plan where 'nothing walks with aimless feet'.[5] Few of us perhaps give the same answer on every day, but can it be denied that the answer we usually give will affect profoundly the way we think about men and their communities?

Disadvantages in the lack of an ideology

If a man is biased the least he can do is to expose his prejudices. My own heart and mind incline to the search for extra-terrestrial charts for the earthly journey. The preference will doubtless be revealed in the content of the present chapter. But in addition my own view is that the exponents of the opposing viewpoint are more frequently on their feet in community work today, and that on the whole they express their opinions more eloquently. Indeed, if we narrow the horizon to only one faith, we find Butler's words a useful commentary on the present standing of religion among many community workers. 'It has come, I know not how, to be taken for granted, by many persons, that Christianity is not so much a subject of enquiry; but that it is, now at length, discovered to be fictitious.'[6]

However, we move away from the consideration of one ideology to suggest that there are areas where the lack of any ideology can represent loss as well as gain for community workers. This fact alone has nothing whatever to do with the truth or falseness of any faith or value-system. Philosophical propositions are not true because everybody would like them to be so: nor for that matter, are they necessarily false for the same reason. If they can be tested, it is elsewhere. But if through lack of attention to ideological matters, there is loss of power in community work, then those employed in this way ought to be among the first to be aware of it. And we maintain there is such a loss.

First there is the phenomenon already suggested that many

people do in fact have spiritual needs. We are often told today that we live in a secular age and certainly the ancient faiths appear to have lost their hold upon the hearts and minds of many of our contemporaries. Yet we cannot fail to notice the popularity of 'faith substitutes', belief systems which are accepted to fill the vacuum. Interest in the occult is growing among all age groups in this country and astrology claims many devotees. A prejudiced view might be that superstition grows when religion declines. Many people find that 'ordinary' events clamour for ultimate explanations. A baby has been born to a family. Who and what is this child? An unwanted encumbrance? A link in the evolutionary chain? A new citizen for the State? A unique creation capable of inheriting eternal values? Ludicrous as these hopes appear to many observers, they do in our opinion represent the unarticulated aspirations of many of the citizens with whom community workers are involved.

If we were right about this, then we might go on to analyse further these spiritual needs. However vaguely, people want to know, (a) that each individual life has ultimate value:[7]

> That not one life shall be destroyed
> Or cast as rubbish to the void

(b) that each individual life has meaning:[8]

> Thou madest man he knows not why
> He thinks he was not made to die

and (c) that the universe is friendly to our noblest endeavours:[9]

> The stars in their courses fought against Siserah.

The argument here is not that these hopes are justified. Our best hopes may in the end prove to be dupes. But we are maintaining that however vague and unformed, they exist in the minds of many of the clientele of the community worker and failure to take account of them may be a loss. Zweig, for example, in his investigation found that religious experiences were far more widespread among the population than is commonly supposed.[10]

Altogether my studies have convinced me that religion in Britain is far from being dead. It is still a vital force with many, I would say, one in four, while the need for religion,

the need to believe is still more widely spread. . . . My
investigations suggest that religious experience is something
common, anyway much more common than we assume, but the
fact is that it rarely comes to the surface. Practically everyone
keeps the secret to himself, one because he cannot express it,
another because he is afraid that his friends will be unable to
understand him, will laugh at him or regard him as queer;
still another may, when the critical time has passed, only half-
believe it or regard it as self-deception.

Frequently we stumble on these mystical commitments in
surprising places, partly because we only expect to find them
associated with membership of a religious organization or ad-
herence to a formal creed. One lesson the present writer learned
as a community worker is that conscious belief is by no means
always the same as unconscious belief. What we think we hold to
is by no means always the same as the subconscious assumptions
which guide our behaviour. In his autobiography Lord Snell told
of the reactions of two visitors one summer to the sudden on-
slaught of a breathtakingly beautiful panoramic view on a Swiss
mountain path. The first, a well-known agnostic, shouted at the
top of his voice: 'Glory! Hallelujah!' The second, an Anglo-
Catholic bishop, muttered: 'Well, I'll be damned.'[11]
    We must not suppose, of course, that these spiritual aspirations
are confined to the unsophisticated and uneducated. We find
J. B. Priestley, for example, driven to paradoxical statements
because he is honestly struggling with his own felt needs and the
paucity of evidence for the satisfaction of those needs.[12]

Religion alone can carry the load, defend us against the
dehumanization collectives, restore true personality. And it is
doubtful if our society can live much longer without
religion. . . . But I have no religion, most of my friends have no
religion. . . . Man lives, under God in a great mystery.

It was Bertrand Russell, no less, who expressed this longing in
language that is not easily forgotten.[13]

The centre of me is always and eternally a terrible pain—a
curious morbid pain—a searching for something beyond what
the world contains, something transfigured and infinite—the
beatific vision of God—I do not find it, and do not think it

is to be found—but the love of it is my life—it's like the passionate love for a ghost.

And in the testament he left, recorded on the last page of his three-volume autobiography, there is a touching passage which should further endear this prophet to the people of this century. It shows that he who had concluded that the best hope man had for progress was to build on the rock of an unyielding despair, still had moments when he trusted that the universe was not implacably opposed to noble endeavour.[14]

I may have thought the road to a world of free and happy human beings shorter than it is proving to be, but I was not wrong in thinking that such a world is possible, and that it is worth while to live with a view to bringing it nearer. I have lived in the pursuit of a vision both personal and social. Personal: to care for what is noble, for what is beautiful, for what is gentle: to allow moments of insight to give wisdom at more mundane times. Social: to see in imagination the society that is to be created, where individuals grow freely, and where hate and greed and envy die because there is nothing to nourish them. These things I believe, and the world, for all its horrors has left me unshaken.

In a related sphere, many philosophers have judged that we cannot answer satisfactorily the question, 'What is education for?' until we have grappled with a previous question, 'What is life for?' 'We believe that education cannot stop short of recognizing the ideals of truth and beauty and goodness as final and binding for all times and in all places as ultimate values.'[15] 'What is the aim of education is a question that admits of no answer without a reference to ultimate convictions about human nature and destiny, about society and how the individual stands related to it.'[16]

So our case is that these questions about an 'ideology' cannot be simply disregarded: whatever our answers may be they are real questions if only because they concern a significant and representative section of the people.

More than that, the lack of an ideology leads to a loss of power and inspiration. A world-view offers the spiritual basis of community. It suggests the like-mindedness which makes people feel that they belong to each other. Lacking this in the present state of anomie, community workers sometimes give the impression that they are trying to make bricks without straw. Muslims have a shared identity with other Muslims: the same is true of Jews. But what is the shared identity of the thousands who live in London? Many would say it is simply our shared humanity, but if that is the right answer it does not appear to be accepted widely enough for our purpose.[17]

We live in a period when the 'existentialist' experience, the feeling of total 'shipwreck' is no longer the exclusive prerogative of extraordinarily sensitive poets and philosophers. Instead, it has become the last shared experience, touching everyone in the whole society, though only a few are able to express it effectively.

Lacking the spiritual basis we often lack also the rituals by which community feeling is both expressed and reinforced. Men have shown a need not only for a sense of common purpose with their fellows but also for the constant dramatization of that purpose. But the ceremonials corresponded to something real in the theology, mythology and psychology of the group. The modern dilemma and deprivation has been put by Fromm.[18]

The need for ritual is undeniable and vastly underestimated. . . . If rituals could be easily devised new humanistic ones might be created. . . . But rituals cannot be manufactured. They depend on the existence of genuinely shared common values, and only to the extent to which such values emerge and become part of human reality can we expect the emergence of meaningful and rational rituals.

Then there are two practical areas in which the lack of an undergirding philosophy proves debilitating. The first is that it tempts the community worker to evade decisions which have to be made on ideological grounds. He may incline to neutrality, avoiding issues in the desire not to risk conflict and dominance, when the matter may touch fundamental human rights. Some community work has been rightly criticized on the grounds that it has avoided confrontation with centres of power and economic wealth which were at the root of deprivation. These issues would have been well understood within a Marxist frame of meaning. Communities have been known to organize their efforts for

K

community selfishness, gaining something for themselves at the expense of another community. What can the worker do in these circumstances? It is not impossible that he might find himself in an area where there were organized efforts to discriminate against coloured people. Does he lend his support on the grounds that he must contrive to be non-directive, or is his behaviour more likely to be guided by his own sense of what is right or wrong? In the affairs of many modern societies, large and small, painful decisions have to be made on the grounds of priorities, not only because there is a shortage of resources, but because improvement for one group is deterioration for another group. It might be possible to improve the standard of living for the present generation but only at the cost of impoverishment of future generations by further destruction of the earth's resources. Who says that we owe anything to those who come after us in the next century? In Calcutta I was told of a cruel irony. The general improvement in medical services during the past few years in that city has made the problems slightly worse for everybody, since the older people tend to live longer and remain around to share the meagre provender. That result was predictable, yet the decision was made, not only on the grounds that there was a balancing good, but in the belief that whatever the consequence it is right to relieve human suffering whenever we can. That seems the right decision and it was rooted in a philosophy.

Finally, there is often a loss of power and a wastage of opportunities because 'ground-floor' community workers do not explore their ideological differences. Again and again one has encountered conflict and misunderstanding and fragmentation of effort concomitant with a reluctance to admit and examine the fact that somewhere inside themselves the operatives are giving different answers to the ancient question, 'What is man?'[19] There are times when the hopes of integration lie in the ability to distinguish between tactics and strategy, policies and philosophy.

The recurring naïveté of some community workers is appealing but weakening. Even those who strive most strenuously to be 'value-free' are still usually far more subjective in their approach to human affairs than they suppose. One cannot be completely non-judgmental except in moments of intense self-conscious effort. One's own interpretations creep in. Our personal philosophy is part of us: we have internalized its commitments: it cannot be shed like an overcoat with a sudden rise in temperature. Honesty and objectivity consist not in forfeiting our bias completely but in the willingness to expose it to the light of day in open discussion. Failure at this point often results in an inability to give identity and location to the 'spanner in the works of colleagueship and co-ordination'. If men cannot agree at least they need to know where and how they differ in order to continue working happily together.

The present discussion could be thought to hinge on the double meaning of the word 'myth'. One interpretation is that 'myth' refers to a popular idea which is not in fact true. But another usage is the rationalization and dramatization of our values. This has been described by MacIver. Myths are 'value-impregnated beliefs and notions that men hold, that they live by or live for': they include 'the most penetrating philosophies of life, the most profound intimations of religion': and 'all social relations are myth-born and myth-sustained'.[20]

If this is true, then our suggestion is that somewhere along the line—though not too often—community workers may usefully have discussions in the terms of 'Let me tell you about my myth and then perhaps you will tell me about yours'. The need and value of this kind of exchange is confirmed by the writer's experience, over several years, of being a supervisor and tutor for a group of professional community workers.

It is clear that in this section, we have asked questions to which we do not know the answers, and for which, indeed, there may be no complete answers. The prospects are small in the foreseeable future for a consensus about one 'myth' among community workers. Pluralism will continue in our society, not least among social workers and educationists. What then? Are the present considerations unnecessary and possibly even divisive? Our contention is that they are required for several reasons. We claim that since every man has his 'myth', the understanding of this is demanded both for self-awareness and for good colleagueship. (In practice, on the second grounds, workers who engage in this type of conversation often acquire an added respect for each other and discover that there is a lot of common ground between those who supposed they were diametrically opposed.) The other reason leads us to the subject of the next section. Even in a society of pluralism where there is no longer one socially acceptable 'myth'—

there might be value for the individual worker in deciding what is to be his own personal philosophy.

Value of a personal philosophy

The dangers of an ideological approach to all forms of service for our fellow men have been well documented. The 'man with a mission' can be a great nuisance. He is preoccupied with the search for the Great Pearl and has no eyes for the lesser pearls.[21] He may look at his fellow men through spectacles tinted by the colour of his own 'myth' and so he may never see them as they truly are. He has his own version of what their needs are and hence he may not listen carefully to their own demands. He can project his own experience on to everybody else and read every human experience in the light of his own. At his worst he is authoritarian in method, divisive in practice and he inhibits educational processes.

All this and more is true. It behoves an advocate in this realm to show himself aware of the formidable arguments against the propositions and the dangers of his arguments being taken too seriously.

In truth, the community worker who looks for a personal philosophy to support his efforts, walks a tight rope. On the one hand he looks for a world-view which expresses more than his personal preferences: which comes to him with the force of 'given and inescapable truth': that therefore in some senses is true for other men as well as for himself, is 'universal' and not merely 'individual'. On the other hand, he should remain open to other men's 'truth': recognize that his 'certainties' are consistent with wide areas of agnosticism: accept that the symbols of expression he uses for his 'truth' may not always be accurate: admit that he does not have the whole truth or hold what he has infallibly: be eager to identify areas of ideological agreement with others rather than constantly be on the look-out for dissonance.

There is a parallel in the way the historic creeds of Christendom have been understood at least by some believers. They grewout of a desire to exclude error as much as the wish to propound a complete and final definition. And so to some they have meant, 'When the final truth is known it will be found to include this and be at least as great as this.'

One is asking here only for a discussion in which we consider whether we have not too prematurely concluded that the personal philosophy of the community worker is an irrelevant survival of a bygone age. Certainly in some quarters it is taken for granted that only the uncommitted can be good social workers or educationists. Perhaps it is time to give attention to the contrary proposition that the rootless may plant few trees.

The issue has been thoughtfully expressed by Lawrence Stenhouse.[22]

In studying the material and the social world as object man is concerned to predict and control. Essentially, he is a determinist looking for causes which explain the patterns of occurrences. In studying his subjective experience of the material and social environment, man is concerned with the purposes and perceptions that can give patterns to choices. He ceases to be a determinist, and regards himself as a responsible actor capable of initiating events. There is no real paradox here. When one takes a subjective point of view, one is merely recognizing the limitations and shortcomings of the determinist frame of reference which is employed to support objectivity. When one takes the objective viewpoint, one is likewise acknowledging the limitations imposed upon subjective purposes by environmental situations over which one cannot gain control.

Granted the difficulties and dangers in the community worker's possession of a world-view, there are obvious advantages in two areas if he gains this by honestly following the argument where it leads.

One is in the realm of his own mental health and emotional strength. A 'faith' can be to the worker a constant source of inspiration, renewal and encouragement. Few people outside the service can have any idea of the heavy demands that are constantly made upon the emotional strength of locally based community workers. There are huge withdrawals upon their capital of hopefulness. Community work does not commonly provide quick and tangible results. There is strength for some at least in being able to fall back occasionally upon the conviction that one is part of something bigger that is an inalienable part of reality. Not without significance is the fact that two of the main contenders for the allegiance of modern man have promised the assurance of final victory to their devotees. Marxism sees the classless society as inevitable though long delayed. Christianity promises the Second Coming of Christ despite the vicissitudes of history.

A personal faith can be part of the renewal system of the over-burdened community worker, though admittedly there are others, like listening to Mozart's music late at night. There are instances when the seriousness of the lack of 'an invisible means of support' is self-evident. One worker in a mood of depression near to breakdown confessed to me that she felt confronted by 'a black, empty nothingness'. One also meets occasionally the worker who is over-intense, over-moralistic, constantly task-related and managerial because he feels that everything depends on his efforts. He does not feel supported by unseen spiritual forces, whether divine or human.

The second gain can be in the way in which he sees and does the work. Whatever interpretations his colleagues hold to, his 'faith' is likely to give him a basis for the unity of human beings, which is supranational—as in the case of the Communist rallying-cry, 'Workers of the world unite'—or supramundane—as in the case of a mystical or religious definition.

There are grounds for supposing that the strongest bases for community are spiritual, that other hopes prove to be shallow and schemes which rely on them alternate between utopianism and despair. We must do the best we can with the materials at our disposal, but community work is often a conscious effort at co-operation among a people who are not impressed by their like-mindedness. It does not well up from unconscious levels but often is a piece of conscious social engineering. Community projects will, to a degree, create community feeling among those taking part. But we are not alone in thinking that the search for a base for our community feeling is not a waste of time and will issue in more effective community projects. 'We know, and we can effectively communicate with other minds, because behind us all there is the common life which holds us together as a unity in diversity—a true unity in a true diversity.'[23]

There have been and are many human occasions when the appeal to a 'mythology of human solidarity' is a powerful resting upon unconscious drives rather than conscious rationalizations. Conversely, many situations illustrate the ancient saying, 'Where there is no vision, the people perish'[24] or 'run amok' as one trans-lation would have it. Gandhi gave a vision to the Indian village people that stressed their dignity, offered them hope and encouraged the co-operation which did something to change their conditions. Laurens van der Post has written of experiencing the 'togetherness' of the Russian people at a circus in Rostov where the workers danced together between the acts. 'It was, I am certain, a significantly Russian evening, woven of the authentic stuff of the national Russian spirit, and it did for the community what I have seen the great tribal dances do for primitive communities in Africa.'[25]

We have already admitted that there does not seem to be available a 'myth for community' which would be acceptable and powerful today, certainly not on an international scale, and perhaps not in a patriotic dimension for developed industrial societies. But that should not prevent us from pointing to the culpable neglect of the emotional bases for community among the writers and practitioners of the subject. The various reports, erudite and professional though they be, have nothing to say about poetry, drama, music and precious little about philosophy.

There might be a case then for the individual community operative working at his own 'faith' and deciding why he thinks that men belong to each other. Whatever his answer, such a one will not want to push it down the throats of his colleagues. He will not want to talk about it all the time. It will certainly not inhibit him from working by professional standards. But whatever is happening to those around him, and however severe the setbacks, he has discovered a powerful reinforcement of his daily efforts.

A Christian interpretation

The choice of Christianity as one ideology for more detailed treatment is not of course fortuitous. There is the writer's own commitment. More important is the fact that there is still a sense in which Britain could be called a 'Christian country'. Some Jeremiahs think we are living in 'the post-Christian era'; though for others who agree with the phrase it evokes a paean of thanksgiving. Just how far the process of secularization has gone in Britain is matter for proper debate. There are those who think it has been much exaggerated by Bryan Wilson[26] and others. David Martin wittily rebuts what he regards as the illogicality of many fashionable statements suggesting that religion is discredited and outmoded.[27] At this point however, the argument develops a curious oscillation. Religion is nowadays very weak but practically all the unpleasant and retrogressive things in our world . . . are due to it. If forces unite people they may 'seem' to be religious but are in fact social, but if they divide people as in India and Pakistan they are really religious. The religious Samson has clearly lost his hair but is incapable of bringing the house down.

It is possible however for us to stay out of this argument and still make the point we want. Whatever stage of secularization has been reached, there are undeniable aspects of life in Britain which justify the choice of the Christian religion as our example. Church and State are linked: the Bible is taught in the schools: a sizeable section of the population are baptized, married and buried by the church: the present inhabitants of these islands are not un-influenced by the part played by Christianity in the growth of their culture, as their daily thought-forms often show.

What is being attempted here is fraught with so many possibili-ties of misunderstanding that we should say clearly what the objectives are: and we begin by saying what is not being attempted.

There is no suggestion here that only those holding the Christian faith can be good community workers. That ludicrous position would be untenable even on the most literal interpretation of the Bible which recognizes that God has many blind servants. 'I girded thee when thou didst not know me',[28] said God to Cyrus, a pagan Emperor. 'O Assyrian, the rod of mine anger';[29] 'I have not found so great faith, no, not in Israel', commented Jesus on a Gentile soldier.[30]

Hence we are not concerned to deny that what is patently true, that other ideologies may supply the support and rationale of community aspirations. Judaism for example is deeply concerned with community, though some would regard its ethnic restrictions as particularistic. Again, we can measure this theologically against what many would regard as the extravagant claims of the Christian faith. The view that the Gospel represents a unique revelation, far from denying truth in other religions, establishes it,

since it affirms that man's search for God has been directed to a
Living God who has answered.

On the level of daily behaviour, we are far from suggesting that
Christians in community work should always be thinking about
their religion and still less always talking about it. The former case
represents 'religiosity' rather than faith. In the second example,
they will certainly not be acceptable to their colleagues. During
recent years there has been a recognition in theological circles that
the totally committed Christian often serves God best by tempo-
rarily forgetting about Him, whilst being concerned with Creation
and absorbed in secular tasks.

It goes without saying that we are not here concerned with this
or that particular doctrine, or denominational preference for a
theological doctrine, or ethical practice, or a ritualist observance.
We focus on a general disposition to interpret the human scene
in the light of the Gospel's view of God, man and society.

Positively, we have two objectives in what follows. One is to
explain to non-believing colleagues the nature of a Christian
involvement in community work. The second is to argue that it is
wholly consistent with their belief for Christians to be involved in
community work: nay, more. Such involvement is the inescapable
logic of their faith on the twentieth-century scene, and this would
be true whether they see Christianity primarily as an ethical system
or an unveiling of eternal verities. The argument is that the New
Testament view of God, man and society is not only conducive
to the aspirations of community but requires them. The church
should exist for the 'world' as well as for itself: it has to be
concerned not only with strengthening its own organizations, but
in fostering community feelings and effort in the society at large.

To those who can believe it, the Christian faith provides
rationale and resources for those who engage in community work.
It insists on the worth of the individual life because of its value to
God. This is proclaimed in the New Testament by extravagant
metaphor. 'The very hairs of your head are all numbered.'[31] One
suspects that the lost sheep was sought not for sentimental reasons
but because it was a valuable piece of property.[32]

As a consequence, we find in the New Testament that people are
treated with respect; they are not 'hustled': their thought-
processes and powers of decision are fully respected in a way that
is wholly consistent with the methods of community development.

'Let every man be fully persuaded in his own mind',[33] is a characteristic statement. The rich young ruler[34] is presented with the demand to give away his possessions to gain inner freedom, but when he cannot accept those terms, no attempt is made to over-persuade him, he is simply allowed to go away. If it is not too contrived an analogy, there is a parallel between the methods of community development and the central affirmation of Christian theology. The former insists that we work *with* and not *for* people: the latter says that in the Incarnation, God came to be *with* us.

Furthermore, the Bible stresses the solidarity of the human race, not on ethnic or other particularist grounds, but for a universal, spiritual reason. 'For this cause, I bow my knees unto the Father of our Lord Jesus Christ of whom the whole family in heaven and earth is named.'[35] 'There is neither Jew nor Greek, there is neither bond nor free: there is neither male nor female.'[36] Hence the Bible, from one perspective, is the record of the search for a community: it knows nothing of a solitary religion but only of believers who are in fellowship with other believers.

The Christian doctrine of 'original sin' has been much misunderstood. It is usually interpreted as pessimism to the point of morbidity and neurosis. But may it not turn out to be 'good news'? It accepts the fallibilities of human nature but without a loss of hope: it knows that men are 'evil' but insists that they are not irredeemable. One sometimes encounters naïve and optimistic community workers who lack this realistic recognition and they are profoundly shaken by the apathy or greed or self-centredness or stupidity of men. There is a vivid illustration of this in Alinsky's *The Professional Radical*. 'Some of the fruit ranchers in California steam around in Cadillacs and treat the Mexican American field hands like vermin. Know who those bastards are? They're the characters who rode west in Steinbeck's trucks in *Grapes of Wrath*.'[37]

Finally, not of least importance, is the renewal of the worker's hope and strength through Christian faith. Through the classic rhythm of repentance, confession, faith and forgiveness, he is constantly 'made anew' to face the considerable demands of his office.

It should be stressed again that throughout this catalogue, we are talking not about formal acceptance of a creed, but about an unconscious and spontaneous disposition to regard the human scene in the light of a Christian interpretation.

We have sought no more in this chapter than more discussion among community workers about the personal ideologies which inform their commitment. This calls for openness and the willingness to listen to contrary views and the humility to know that we have much to learn from each other. Fundamental ideological differences need not always result in estrangement and conflict. They can lead to respect, better understanding and colleagueship: above all, they may help some of us to find the emotional bases of community.

Notes

1 What is a community?

1 M. R. Mitford, *Our Village*, Dent, 1951 edition, p. 3.
2 G. A. Hillary, 'Definitions of community: areas of agreement', *Rural Sociology*, 1955, 20, pp. 111–23. Part of the confusion arises from the fact that we do not in our language have different words to describe community in general (*Gemeinschaft*) and local community (*Gemeinde*).
3 R. Redfield, *The Little Community: Viewpoints for the Study of a Human Whole*, University of Chicago Press, 1955.
4 Ronald Blythe, *Akenfield*, Penguin, 1969.
5 Ronald Goldman, *Angry Adolescents*, Routledge & Kegan Paul, 1969.
6 R. König, *The Community*, Routledge & Kegan Paul, 1968, pp. 40–1.
7 Ibid., p. 28.
8 G. Duncan Mitchell, *A Dictionary of Sociology*, Routledge & Kegan Paul, 1968, p. 32.
9 Cf. Kingsley Davis, *Human Society*, Macmillan, ch. 12.
10 Ibid.
11 F. Tönnies, *Community and Association*, Routledge & Kegan Paul, 1955.
12 R. M. MacIver, *Society*, Macmillan, 1937.
13 É. Durkheim, *The Division of Labour in Society*, Free Press, 1964.
14 C. H. Cooley, *Social Organization*, Scribner, 1909.
15 Peter Worsley (ed.), *Introducing Sociology*, Penguin, 1970, pp. 262 ff.

2 What is community development?

1 Murray G. Ross and B. W. Lappin, *Community Organization: Theory and Principles*, Harper, 1955, pp. 23 ff.
2 *Community Work and Social Change: A Report on Training*, Longmans, 1968.
3 Professor Nathan E. Cohen in *International Social Work*, 1968 (yearbook), p. 58.
4 Sir Fred Clarke, 'The social functions of secondary education', *Sociological Review*, July/October 1971.
5 Timothy Raison (ed.), *The Founding Fathers of Social Science*, Penguin, p. 94.
6 P. Kropotkin, *Mutual Aid*, Heinemann, 1902, ch. 8.
7 *Report of the Committee on Local Authority and Allied Personal Social Services*, HMSO, 1968.
8 Ross, in op. cit., p. 14.
9 Gulbenkian Foundation, *Current Issues in Community Work: A*

Study by the Community Work Group, Routledge & Kegan Paul, 1973.
10 C. D. Poster, *The School and the Community*, Macmillan, 1971.
11 Ibid., p. 17.
12 Reported in Ross and Lappin, op. cit., pp. 9 ff.
13 Margaret Mead in *Community Education*, ed. C. O. Arndt, University of Chicago Press, 1959, p. 74.
14 Cf. the suggestions for further reading and study at the end of this book.

3   The work of the community developers

1 *Community Work and Social Change*, Longmans, 1968.
2 George W. Goetschius, *Working With Community Groups*, Routledge & Kegan Paul, 1969.
3 Murray G. Ross, *Case Histories in Community Organization*, Harper, 1958, pp. 164–91.
4 Ibid., p. 175.
5 Ibid., p. 191.
6 *Report of the Working Party on Police Training in Race Relations*, HMSO, 1971.
7 B. R. Wilson, 'The teachers' role—a sociological analysis', *British Journal of Sociology*, 1962, 13.
8 J. B. Mays, *Education and the Urban Child*, University of Liverpool Press, 1962.
9 Ibid.
10 W. G. A. Rudd and S. Wiseman, 'Sources of dissatisfaction among a group of teachers', *British Journal of Educational Psychology*, 1962, 32.
11 Catherine Lindsay, *School and Community*, Pergamon, 1971, p. 119.
12 Frank Musgrove and Philip H. Taylor, *Society and the Teachers' Role*, Routledge & Kegan Paul, 1969, p. 67.
13 H. E. Bracey, *Neighbours*, Routledge & Kegan Paul, 1964.
14 Quoted by Sir Fred Clarke, *Freedom in the Educative Society*, University of London Press, 1948.
15 Margaret Mead, *Growing up in New Guinea*, Penguin, 1942, pp. 207–8.
16 *Educational Priorities*, HMSO, 1972.
17 A. N. Gillett, 'Teachers for community schools—a comparative viewpoint', in *Towards a Policy for Teachers' Education*, ed. W. Taylor, Butterworth, 1969.

4   The skill and training of the community worker

1 M. Argyle, *The Psychology of Interpersonal Behaviour*, Penguin, 1967.
2 Fred Milson, *An Introduction to Group Work Skill*, Routledge & Kegan Paul, 1973.

3 Roland L. Warren, *The Community in America*, Rand McNally, 1963, p. 165.
4 W. J. H. Sprott, *Human Groups*, Penguin, 1958, ch. 8.
5 John Leigh, *Young People and Leisure*, Routledge & Kegan Paul, 1971.
6 Cf. the account of the Hawthorne industrial experiment in George C. Homans, *The Human Group*, Routledge & Kegan Paul, 1951.
7 Gulbenkian report, *Community Work and Social Change*, Longmans, 1968, p. 128.
8 Ibid., pp. 146 and 151.

5 Why the present interest in community work?

1 'The world poverty problem', *Encyclopedia Britannica*, Book of the Year, 1972, p. 34.
2 Many examples can be found in: Nelson B. Henry (ed.), *Community Education*, National Society for the Study of Education, 1959.
3 Lawrence Stenhouse, *Culture and Education*, Nelson, 1967, p. 50.
4 *Community Organization*, National Council of Social Service, 1962, p. 10.
5 G. Duncan Mitchell (ed.), *A Dictionary of Sociology*, Routledge & Kegan Paul, 1968, sections on 'Function' and 'Conflict'. Peter Berger, *Invitation to Sociology*, Penguin, 1963, ch. 2.
6 Murray G. Ross and B. W. Lappin, *Community Organization: Theory and Principles*, Harper, 1955, ch. 3.
7 Maurice R. Stein, *The Eclipse of the Community*, Harper, 1960, p. 299.
8 *The Grief Report*, published by Shelter, 1972.
9 George C. Homans, *The Human Group*, Routledge & Kegan Paul, 1951.
10 *Community Work and Social Change*, Longmans, 1968, p. 80.
11 Quoted in ibid., p. 70.
12 *Youth and Community Work in the '70s*, HMSO, 1969, p. 59.
13 Max Weber (trans. and ed. by H. H. Gerth and C. Wright Mills), *Essays in Sociology*, Oxford University Press, 1946, ch. on 'Bureaucracy', p. 244.
14 Ronald Frankenberg, *Communities in Britain*, Penguin, 1966, p. 285.
15 Charles A. Reich, *The Greening of America*, Penguin, 1970.
16 'To John Driden of Chesterton', *Epistles*, I. i.
17 Weber, op. cit.
18 Peter Worsley (ed.), *Modern Sociology. Introductory Readings*, Penguin, 1970, ch. 54.
19 Peter Worsley (ed.), *Introducing Sociology*, Penguin, 1970, p. 45.
20 Ibid., ch. 5.
21 Peter Black, *The Biggest Aspidistra in the World*, BBC, 1972, p. 215.
22 J. Spencer, *Stress and Release in an Urban Estate: A Study of Action Research*, Tavistock, 1964.
23 *New Society*, 2 January 1969.

6 The values of community work

1 The word is a translation from the German *wertfrei* and the theory was advanced by Weber. Cf. article on Max Weber in G. Duncan Mitchell (ed.), *A Dictionary of Sociology*, Routledge & Kegan Paul, 1968.

2 Maurice R. Stein, *The Eclipse of the Community*, Harper, 1960, p. 283.

3 *Community Work and Social Change*, Longmans, 1968, p. 78.

4 Colin Bell and Howard Newby, *Community Studies*, Allen & Unwin, 1971, pp. 16 and 17.

5 Quoted from Murray G. Ross and B. W. Lappin, *Community Organization: Theory and Principles*, Harper, 1955, pp. 83–4.

6 A. K. C. Ottaway, *Education and Society*, Routledge & Kegan Paul, 1953, p. 85.

7 Gulbenkian report, *Community Work and Social Change*, Longmans, 1968, p. 79.

8 Ronald Blythe, *Akenfield*, Penguin, 1969, pp. 118–19.

9 Glen Leef, 'The united national program of community development', ch. 16 in Nelson B. Henry (ed.), *Community Education*, National Society for the Study of Education, 1959.

10 Num. 14:2.

11 Deut. 1:40.

12 H. E. Bracey, *Neighbours*, Routledge & Kegan Paul, 1964, p. 179.

13 Roger Wilson, *Difficult Housing Estates*, Tavistock, 1963, pp. 3 and 9.

14 Ross and Lappin, op. cit., p. 212.

15 W. W. Biddle, *Encouraging Community Development*, Holt, Rinehart & Winston, 1968, p. 79.

16 Ibid., p. 29.

17 Ibid., p. 85.

18 *Community Organization*, National Council of Social Service, 1962, p. 58 and Biddle, op. cit., pp. 140–1 and 148–9.

19 Quoted from *Penguin Dictionary of Modern Quotations*, 1971, p. 251.

20 T. L. Green, 'Lessons in community education learned through technical assistance programs', ch. 9 in Henry, op. cit.

21 B. Bernstein, 'Social class and linguistic development: a theory of social learning', in A. H. Halsey, J. Floud and C. A. Anderson (eds), *Education, Economy and Society*, Free Press, 1961, pp. 288–314.

22 Brian Jackson and Dennis Marsden, *Education and the Working Class*, Penguin, 1966.

23 Lawrence Stenhouse, *Culture and Education*, Nelson, 1967, pp. 76–7.

24 Mary Morse, *The Unattached*, Penguin, 1965, p. 40.

25 Paul Halmos, *Faith of the Counsellors*, Constable, 1965.

26 Lord Moran, *Winston Churchill: The Struggle for Survival 1940–1965*, Constable, 1966.

7 The faith of the community worker

1 Maurice R. Stein, *The Eclipse of the Community*, Harper, 1960, p. 295.
2 W. W. Biddle, *Encouraging Community Development*, Holt, Rinehart & Winston, 1968, pp. 31–2.
3 Albert Camus, *The Rebel*, ch. I.
4 Samuel Taylor Coleridge, *The Ancient Mariner*, part I.
5 Alfred, Lord Tennyson, *In Memoriam*, liv.
6 Bishop Butler, *The Analogy of Religion*, 1756, advertisement.
7 Tennyson, op. cit., liv.
8 Ibid.
9 Judg. 5:20.
10 F. Zweig, *The Quest for Fellowship*, Heinemann, 1965, pp. 123–4.
11 Lord Snell, *Men, Movements and Myself*, Dent, 1936, pp. 164–5.
12 J. B. Priestley, *Literature and Western Man*, Mercury, 1962, pp. 357–8.
13 *The Autobiography of Bertrand Russell 1914–1944*, Allen & Unwin, 1968, p. 75.
14 Ibid., p. 223.
15 *The Curriculum and Examinations in Schools* (Norwood Report), HMSO, 1943, p. 55.
16 *Secondary Education*, HMSO, 1947, p. 9.
17 Stein, op. cit., p. 329.
18 Erich Fromm, *Psychoanalysis and Religion*, Yale University Press, 1950, pp. 110–11.
19 Ps. 8:4.
20 R. M. MacIver, *The Web of Government*, Macmillan, 1947, p. 4.
21 Matt. 13:45–6.
22 Lawrence Stenhouse, *Culture and Education*, Nelson, 1967, pp. 95–6.
23 Werner Stark, *The Fundamental Forms of Social Thought*, Routledge & Kegan Paul, 1962, p. 228.
24 Prov. 29:18.
25 Laurens van der Post, *Journey into Russia*, Hogarth, 1964, pp. 35–6.
26 Bryan Wilson, *Religion in Secular Society*, Penguin, 1969.
27 David Martin, *The Religious and the Secular*, Routledge & Kegan Paul, 1969, p. 66.
28 Isa. 45:5.
29 Isa. 10:5.
30 Luke 7:9.
31 Matt. 10:30.
32 Luke 15:3–7.
33 Rom. 14:5.
34 Matt. 19:16–22.
35 Eph. 3:14–15.
36 Gal. 3:28.
37 Marion K. Sanders, *Professional Radical: Conversations with Saul Alinsky*, Harper & Row, 1970.

L

Suggestions for further reading and study

The present work is introductory, a primer for the study of community work: it should be judged as such. But for those readers who wish to carry the subject further, the outline of a course for subsequent reading and study replaces the usual bibliography. Through this scheme, issues which were raised in the text, but dealt with cursorily due to the exigencies of space, can be examined in depth. In addition, important issues are referred to in this outline which have found no mention in the text.

An asterisk denotes a book which, in the opinion of the author, is more difficult to understand than the rest. It should not, of course, be avoided on that account. Close attention and careful study may prove particularly rewarding in these cases. But the writer's experience as a tutor has demonstrated how easily students can be discouraged by early encounter with a book they find difficult to understand.

1 What is a community?

From a sociological perspective this is the most theoretical chapter in the book. There are three underlying issues, (a) Is 'community' a sociological reality or is it only a method of enquiry? (b) If it is such a reality, in what categories may it be described, for example geography or interest? (c) How much have communities been affected by modern conditions? There are many volumes on these issues but perhaps they can be divided into two types. The first is general studies. The second is community studies with attempts at conceptualizing conclusions or theoretical works which rely very heavily on community studies. (Yet a third type is the community study which makes no theoretical pretensions, but is sometimes written almost like a historical novel or mass-media documentary.) Such works may be of less value for the serious student but they are of greater interest to a wider public.

General studies

*König, René, *The Community*, Routledge & Kegan Paul, 1968.
*Tönnies, F., *Community and Association*, Routledge & Kegan Paul, 1955.
*Warren, Roland L., *The Community in America*, Rand McNally, 1963, chs 1 and 2.

Worsley, Peter (ed.), *Introducing Sociology*, Penguin, 1970, ch. 6, 'The community in modern Britain'.

Theoretical works relying heavily upon community studies

*Bell, Colin and Newby, Howard, *Community Studies*, Allen & Unwin, 1971.
Frankenberg, R., *Communities in Britain*, Penguin, 1966.
Klein, Josephine, *Samples from British Culture*, Routledge & Kegan Paul, 1965.
Stein, Maurice R., *The Eclipse of the Community*, Harper, 1960.

Community studies of the 'heavier' kind

Arensberg, C. A. and Kimball, S. T., *Family & Community in Ireland*, Oxford University Press, 1968.
Davis, Allison, Gardner, Burleigh B. and Gardner, Mary R., *Deep South*, University of Chicago Press, 1941.
Dennis, N., Henriques, F. and Slaughter, C., *Coal is our Life*, Eyre & Spottiswoode, 1969.
Dollard, John, *Caste and Class in a Southern Town*, Doubleday, 1957.
Emmett, Isabel, *A North Wales Parish*, Routledge & Kegan Paul, 1964.
Frankenberg, R., *Village on the Border*, Cohen & West, 1957.
Littlejohn, J., *Westrigg : The Sociology of a Cheviot Parish*, Routledge & Kegan Paul, 1964.
Lynd, R. S. and Lynd, H. M., *Middletown*, Harcourt, Brace & World, 1929.
Lynd, R. S. and Lynd, H. M., *Middletown in Transition*, Harcourt, Brace & World, 1937.
Mogey, J. M., *Family and Neighbourhood*, Oxford University Press, 1956.
*Park, R. E., *Human Communities*, Free Press, 1952.
Rees, A., *Life in a Welsh Countryside*, Free Press, 1950.
Seely, J. R., Sim, R. A. and Loosley, E. W., *Crestwood Heights*, Wiley, 1963.
Stacey, M., *Tradition and Change: A Study of Banbury*, Oxford University Press, 1960.
*Vidich, R., Max, J. and Bensman, Joseph, *Small Town in Mass Society*, Princeton University Press, 1958.
Ware, Caroline C., *Greenwich Village*, Houghton Mifflin, 1935.
Williams, W. M., *The Sociology of an English Village*, Routledge & Kegan Paul, 1956.
Wirth, Louis, *The Ghetto*, University of Chicago Press, 1928.

Community studies of a more 'readable' kind

Blythe, Ronald, *Akenfield*, Penguin, 1969.
Williams, Raymond, *Border Country*, Penguin, 1962.
Young, Michael and Willmott, Peter, *Family and Kinship in East London*, Routledge & Kegan Paul, 1957.

For the issue that the 'local community' is still a significant part of the individual's experience, cf. König, op. cit.

For a critical assessment of the different research methods used by 'community investigators' cf. Bell and Newby, op. cit., ch. 3.

For an invaluable discussion of many of the basic issues in this chapter cf. Mann, P. H., *An Approach to Urban Sociology*, Routledge & Kegan Paul, 1965.

Study in this area will be facilitated by a dictionary of sociology.

Highly recommended and cheap in price is Mitchell, G. Duncan (ed.), *A Dictionary of Sociology*, Routledge & Kegan Paul, 1970 (paperback).

2 What is community development?

There are two main processes for further exploration. One is to read the books which are devoted to descriptions and definitions. A selected list is given below. The second—and on the whole far more readable approach—is to use the accounts of community development projects. But as this area relates equally well to the next chapter the references are given there though they should not be neglected as useful commentaries on the present chapter.

(Another valuable method of understanding is to be personally involved in a community development project, but strictly speaking this recommendation lies outside the present terms of reference.)

Batten, T. R., *The Human Factor in Community Work*, Oxford University Press, 1965.
Batten, T. R., *The Non-Directive Approach in Group and Community Work*, Oxford University Press, 1967.
Biddle, W. W., *The Community Development Process*, Holt, Rinehart & Winston, 1965, ch. 3.
Community Organization: An Introduction, National Council of Social Service, 1962.
Community Work and Social Change (Gulbenkian report), Longmans, 1968.
Henry, Nelson B. (ed.), *Community Education*, National Society for the Study of Education, 1959.

Kramer, Ralph M. and Specht, Harry, *Readings in Community Organization Practice*, Prentice Hall, 1969.
Leaper, R. A. B., *Community Work*, National Council of Social Service, 1968.
Ross, Murray G. and Lappin, B. W., *Community Organization : Theory and Principles*, Harper, 1955.

3 The work of the community developers

Readable accounts of 'grass roots' community-work projects

Community Development Journal, issued monthly by Oxford University Press.
Goetschius, George and Tash, Joan M., *Working with Unattached Youth*, Routledge & Kegan Paul, 1967.
Goetschius, George, *Working with Community Groups*, Routledge & Kegan Paul, 1968.
Henry, Nelson B. (ed.), *Community Education*, National Society for the Study of Education, 1959, section II, chs 6 and 11.
Ross, Murray G., *Case Histories in Community Organization*, Harper, 1958.
(There is as yet a shortage of casework material, notably from the British scene.)

Community work and the teacher

Educational Priorities, HMSO, 1972.
Garforth, F. W., *Education and Social Purpose*, Oldbourne, 1962.
Lindsay, Catherine, *School and Community*, Pergamon, 1971.
Mays, J. B., *Education and the Urban Child*, University of Liverpool Press, 1962.
Musgrove, Frank and Taylor, Philip H., *Society and the Teacher's Role*, Routledge & Kegan Paul, 1969.
Ottaway, A. K. C., *Education and Society*, Routledge & Kegan Paul, 1953.
Poster, C. D., *The School and the Community*, Macmillan, 1971.
Stenhouse, Lawrence, *Culture and Education*, Nelson, 1967.

Students should give some attention to the view that there is in contemporary societies an undue reliance upon the educational establishment. Illich, Reimer, Goodman and Freire advance these strong criticisms. Schools (including colleges and universities) are not nearly efficient enough in the attainment of education for the masses : they are ruinously expensive : and they perpetuate injustice and privilege. It is true that the experience of these writers has usually been in the Third World, the poorer sections of the human family and particularly in South America. Here the argument for 'de-schooling' is at its strongest. For many in developing countries formal education has opened only the windows of opportunity, but not the doors. But all the writers would claim that these arguments also have relevance for developed countries like the USA and Britain. This point of view is particularly interesting for us, since the aim of community development might be stated simply as the emergence of the 'educative society' where we all learn more from daily living than from attendance at educational establishments. A few readable and inexpensive books give a good account of the 'de-schooling' philosophy.

Freire, Paulo, *Cultural Action for Freedom*, Penguin, 1972.
Goodman, Paul, *Compulsory Miseducation*, Penguin, 1971.
Illich, Ivan D., *Celebration of Awareness*, Penguin, 1973.
Illich, Ivan D., *Deschooling Society*, Penguin, 1973.
Reimer, Everett, *School is Dead*, Penguin, 1971.

General issues

The two Gulbenkian reports are the most thoughtful British contribution to a discussion both about the role of the 'grass roots' community developer and also about the relevance of community work for other professions. In particular see:

Community Work and Social Change, Longmans, 1968, ch. 3 'The nature of community work', ch. 6 'The functions of community workers'.
Current Issues in Community Work. Routledge & Kegan Paul, 1973, ch. 3 'Community work methods'; ch. 6 'Community workers and their employers'.

Community work and the church

Lovell, George, *The Church and Community Development: An Introduction*, Grail, 1972.

4 The skill and training of the community worker

The first Gulbenkian report (*Community Work and Social Change*), to which constant reference has already been made, is basic to the subject-matter of this chapter: after all, its sub-title was *A Report on Training*. See, in particular, Part III, chapters 8 and 11.

But this should be read in the light of the second Gulbenkian report (*Current Issues in Community Work*). See in particular chapter 7 on 'Training' and appendix 4 which gives the outlines of some university courses in community work.
On general issues about skill and training, cf. Goetschius, op. cit. More specifically on details of training:

Batten, T. R., *Training for Community Development*, Oxford University Press, 1962.
Biddle, W. W., *Encouraging Community Development. A Training Guide for Local Workers*, Holt, Rinehart & Winston, 1968.
Field Work Supervision for Community Work Students, National Council of Social Service, 1970.
Supervision of Community Work Students, National Council of Social Service, 1969.

Courses

The first Gulbenkian report provides an annotated list of full-time courses in this and other countries. For a list of short courses cf. Lovell, op. cit., pp. 75–6.

5   Why the present interest in community work?

This is a large subject and would require from us a heavy programme of reading in contemporary history, covering both the malaise and the aspirations of our generation. What follows is a selection covering the following considerations:
1 Something wrong with 'communities' today.
2 The need, hope and promise of community work.
3 The relevance of community development for a few specialized areas.

Community Organization, National Council of Social Service, 1962, chs 1–2.
Daniel, W. W., *Racial Discrimination in England*, Penguin, 1968.
Goetschius, George, *Working with Community Groups*, Routledge & Kegan Paul, 1968, ch. 2.
The Grief Report, published by Shelter, 1972.
Gulbenkian report, *Community Work and Social Change*, Longmans, 1968, ch. 2.
Gulbenkian report, *Current Issues in Community Work*, Routledge & Kegan Paul, 1973, ch. 2.

Spencer, J., *Stress and Release in an Urban Estate: A Study of Action Research*, Tavistock, 1964.

Stein, Maurice R., *The Eclipse of the Community*, Harper, 1960, chs 10–12.

Warren, Roland L., *The Community in America*, Rand McNally, 1963.

Williams, Raymond, *The Long Revolution*, Penguin, 1965.

Worsley, Peter (ed.), *Problems of Modern Society*, Penguin, 1973, Parts 2–4.

6 and 7 The values and faith of the community worker

The commonest meaning of 'values' in our discussion is 'the purposes the worker has in mind and which he considers are desirable': that of 'faith' is 'the personal philosophy which in his view supports and validates his chosen goals.' And though these two are separate, it is our argument that usually the two are closely related. They are not strangers and apart. They are constantly and vitally interacting with one another. On this view, they are best studied together.

For the proposition that value assumptions lie behind community work

*Friedrich, Carl J. (ed.), *Community*, Liberal Arts, 1959.

Gulbenkian report, *Community Work and Social Change*, Longmans, 1968, ch. 7.

*Kramer, Ralph M. and Specht, Harry (eds), *Readings in Community Organization Practice*, Prentice Hall, 1969, Section B 12, 'Goals, structures, and strategies for community change', by Martin Rein and Robert Morris.

Stein, Maurice R., *The Eclipse of the Community*, Harper, 1960, ch. 12, 'Sociological perspectives on the modern community'.

For attempts to describe what those value assumptions are

Gulbenkian report, *Current Issues in Community Work*, Routledge & Kegan Paul, 1973, ch. 2.

An Intercultural Exploration. Universals and Differences in Social Work Values, Functions and Practice (Report of the Intercultural Seminar held at the East–West Center, Hawaii, 1966), Council on Social Work Education, New York.

Ross, Murray G., *Case Histories in Community Organization*, Harper 1958, ch. 3.

For attempts to demonstrate the proposition that the Christian faith has peculiar relevance for the value assumptions of community work

*Berger, Peter, *A Rumour of Angels*, Penguin, 1971.
Jeffreys, M. V. C., *Personal Values in the Modern World*, Penguin, 1962.
*Kramer, Ralph M. and Specht, Harry, op. cit., section 'The church and neighbourhood community organization' by Thomas D. Sherrard and Richard C. Murray.
Lovell, George, *The Church and Community Development*, Grail, 1972.
*Martin, David, *The Religious and the Secular*, Routledge & Kegan Paul, 1969.
Milson, Fred, *Church, Youth and Community Development*, Epworth, 1970.

Examples of writers who would disagree with the last proposition

*Bronowski, J., *The Identity of Man*, Penguin, 1967.
*Freud, S., *Civilization and its Discontents*, Hogarth, 1951, vol. 21, 1930.
Russell, Bertrand, *Authority and the Individual*, Reith Lecture, 1949.
*Weber, M., *The Sociology of Religion*, Beacon, 1968.
Wilson, Bryan, *Religion in Secular Society*, Penguin, 1969.

From several perspectives, Erich Fromm is a rewarding writer in the present discussion. He spans both the distinction between values and philosophy, and also between those who do and those who do not find the Christian interpretation helpful. Apparently he does not believe in God in any conventional sense but he finds the Biblical symbols indispensable for an understanding of modern men and their societies.

Fromm, Erich, *Fear of Freedom*, Routledge & Kegan Paul, 1942.
Fromm, Erich, *The Sane Society*, Routledge & Kegan Paul, 1956.

Subject index

151

Author index